Small City Tales of Strangeness and Beauty

Small City Tales of Strangeness and Beauty

Edited by Gillian Britton and Stephen Lawrence

Wakefield
Press

Wakefield Press
1 The Parade West
Kent Town
South Australia 5067
www.wakefieldpress.com.au

First published 2009

Cover design by Michael Deves
Typeset by Wakefield Press
Printed and bound by Hyde Park Press, Adelaide

National Library of Australia Cataloguing-in-Publication entry

Title:	Small city tales of strangeness and beauty/ edited by Gillian Britton, Stephen Lawrence.
ISBN:	978 1 86254 834 3 (pbk.).
Subjects:	Adelaide (S. Aust.).
	Adelaide (S. Aust.) – Anecdotes.
	Adelaide (S. Aust.) – Social life and customs.
Other Authors/Contributors:	Britton, Gillian.
	Lawrence, Stephen.
Dewey Number:	994.231

Contents

Foreword

In the words of the poet Jill Jones, 'What runs through you will get you'. In these stories, poems and photographs with Adelaide as its theme, the city sighs with shifting sands. Its mornings swirl with readdressed mail and untended gardens, its afternoons seethe with melting bitumen and its nights crackle with heat, breakdown, the attrition of marriages. The city disgorges stories in the way waste yields coloured glass, not as a collector's item but as something being halted from passing out of memory. There are some gems here. From a profoundly disabled boy to a confident rapper on a palindrome beach, words withdraw like wounded animals or they run backwards to trumpet love. But home is not quite where the heart is and this anthology gets to the heart of the matter: a small city marks you with exquisite moments of delight and pain. These are candid tales broken open, but they bear honest seeds.

Brian Castro, Chair, Creative Writing, University of Adelaide

Acknowledgements

The editors would like to acknowledge the support of those people most directly responsible for this collection. In particular, we wish to thank Professor Nicholas Jose, former Chair of the Creative Writing Department of the University of Adelaide, for his keen advice on and promotion of the book. And thanks to Michael Bollen and the team at Wakefield Press, who have done so much over many years in support of South Australian writing. And the writers and photographers themselves, for donating their creative time and efforts to this venture.

Editors' Introduction

A region or a way of life does not begin to exist until it has been interpreted by one artist after another.

Nettie Palmer

When the call went out for submissions for an anthology about Adelaide, writers and photographers from around Australia responded, not just inspired by the theme but by its title, *Small City Tales of Strangeness and Beauty*. It struck a chord with people who knew that, as well as hosting world-famous festivals and writers' events, and harbouring understated natural and urbane charms, Adelaide also possesses an underbelly that has succoured some very odd and murderous occurrences.

From these submissions, the editors have chosen works by both new and well-established writers and photographers, some from South Australia, others from further afield. They offer stories, poems and images that begin in the heart of Adelaide – taking us to Rundle Mall, the Central Market, the Christmas Pageant, Hindley Street, North Terrace and the University of Adelaide, city pubs, Rymill Park, the Festival Centre and Writers' Week. Then the tales move to the suburbs, Hills, wine district and Adelaide's beaches.

Small City Tales takes us into the city's past, reflects on its contemporary faces, and even projects us into a chilling future. It tells stories of the displaced, the transplanted, the entrenched and the ambivalent; it tells the tale of this place, in all its strangeness and its beauty.

The city invoked these stories, poems and photographs. In turn, they bring Adelaide to vivid life.

Gillian Britton and Stephen Lawrence, December 2008

Gearing Up

Heather Taylor Johnson

There's some obscure station tuned in
it's funky, instrumental.
Dresses and towels keep rhythm in the breeze
while the pumpkin patch grows like a maze.
Summer, yeah.

Adelaide has 2 seasons:
wet and festival.
Jumper-wrapped and ugg-enclosed, we live like squirrels
hoarding our acorns all winter long so when summer, yeah

when summer comes
we are starving
searching our closets for brightness and what feels light
and we come together without a plan or map to guide us
through the city's streets and we celebrate with mango
dripping down chins, chardonnay sploshing gold-painted glass rims
we celebrate, ravenously, the feast.

A Live Kidney

Petra Fromm

The breeze on North Terrace still held a hint of overnight chill. Jade didn't have a jumper so she walked quickly, thinking how the old buildings on the south side of the road seemed to smell of money. The Botanic Gardens looked beautiful this early, revived overnight from the previous day's heat fatigue. Jade remembered having a family picnic there once, back in the days when her dad was still around. She guessed she would have been about nine and Davey six. He'd refused to eat Mum's soggy cheese and tomato sandwiches so Dad had fed them to the ducks. Instead, he bought Balfours' chocolate frogs and ice-creams, joking that no child in Australia should go hungry. Smiling to herself at the memory, she wished for the millionth time that Dad hadn't left. She hadn't seen Mum or Davey in ages either. She should give them a call. Sometimes she missed Davey so much that it hurt, which always surprised her because he'd been such a pain when he was little, wanting to tag along with her and her friends, getting into her stuff. Maybe she would call them, tonight, or tomorrow.

The traffic had built up while she walked. Surly cars nudged along to the beat of breakfast radio while buses disgorged early risers on their way to air-conditioned offices. Jade slowed her pace a bit; it was starting to warm up and already the sun had a sting in it, predicting another scorching day. She joined the hundreds of young people filtering off North Terrace into Adelaide Uni for the first day of Orientation Week. Funny, she thought, how they dressed for uni, as if they'd waited their whole lives to chuck school uniform for something individual, something that made a statement about who they really were. Jade thought it was a pity so many of them opted for designer-label crap but you saw all sorts; the ones who tried too hard by wearing gear better suited to a club or rave, the ones who got it wrong by trying to look as if they were not trying and rocking up in old track pants. Most of the Asian chicks dressed great though, with a real sense of style. Jade tried to imagine shopping for clothes in Hong Kong or even better, Tokyo.

As always during O Week there was a sausage sizzle breakfast on the Barr Smith Lawns and she stood in the queue, wishing it was out of the sun.

'Can I have two?' she asked the guy putting sausages in bread.

'Nup, one each,' he said, without looking at her.

'Aw, come on mate, don't be a Nazi. Who's gonna know?'

He looked up then, frowning, but she flashed him a smile, saying she'd had a big night and he shrugged, putting two sausages on separate bits of bread.

'You want sauce and onion?'

'Please,' she nodded. 'Cheers mate. Have a good one.' She flashed him the smile again and grabbed a can of Coke, stashing it in her backpack and taking her sausages to a shady spot on the lawns. She wolfed the first one down too quickly and felt like she was going to puke it back up. Meat never agreed with her first thing in the morning so she waited before eating the other one, sipping the Coke while a three-piece band did their sound check on an improvised stage at the other end of the lawns. When she'd eaten the second sausage she stretched out, rested her head on her backpack and let her mind float away with the music.

It must have been hours later when she woke up, sweating. Her lips were cracked and she could feel the tiny bumps of sunburn blisters along the bridge of her nose. While she was asleep the lawns had filled up and people were stepping or tripping over her legs, yelling to their mates over the noise of the band. Staggering to her feet, groggy and dying for a piss, Jade pushed her way across the lawns, through the Cloisters and down the stairs of the Lady Symon Building to the women's toilets. There was a queue here too and she had to clench her pelvic floor muscles tight, counting backwards from a hundred to take her mind off her bladder.

When she came out of the toilet, she washed her hands and face at the basin, slurping a long drink of water from the tap, but she still felt like shit. Her armpits smelt like feral cat so she claimed one of the shower cubicles. Chucking her clothes on the floor, she turned the cold tap on as hard as it would go and forced herself to stand in the stream of water until she was shivering. Shaking herself dry, she got a different T-shirt out of her backpack and rummaged around for clean knickers. No luck there, she'd just have to put her jeans back on without. Glancing in the mirror to flick her hair into place, she was glad now that she'd cut it short. Life was a hell of a lot easier with short hair.

Back on the lawns, Jade looked around for familiar faces but didn't recognise anyone. They were handing out free beer but you had to have an armband and she didn't so she decided to head up to Rundle Mall. By the time she'd climbed the stairs leading back onto North Terrace she was sweating again. The walk up Pulteney Street seemed almost too much effort but Target was worth it. Everyone knew Target had the best air-conditioning in the city; someone had even written a song about it. Halfway there, standing in the court-yard of the Tower Building, was a middle-aged Asian man holding a white placard. He looked tired, she thought. No, he looked sick, his jowly face hanging in grey folds as if holding up the skin was too much effort. He looked beaten. Defeated. Her dad had looked like that after he lost his job, back when he and Mum were still trying to find a way to keep the house. Keep the family together. Jade looked at the words on the placard, written in wide black marker:

I WISH TO DONATE A LIVE KIDNEY

What the fuck? Jade kept walking, trying not to stare. But she couldn't help wondering what was going on. It didn't look like a joke. What did he mean by DONATE; did he want to give away a kidney or was he trying to sell it? Were people even allowed to do that here? There were a lot of weirdos around but she thought this one had to be either a complete nut-job or someone in real trouble.

Pushing her way through the crowd in the doorway of Target, she leaned against the wall and stared over heads in the pretence that she was waiting for someone. They'd ask you to move away if you weren't there to shop. As the cool air wrapped around her, she thought about the Asian man and his kidney, wondering what the deal was, wishing she'd had the guts to go up and ask him. But what could you say? *Are you for real?* Or how about *Hang on a minute while I run home for my kidney dish.* She laughed aloud at the weakness of her own joke, attracting the attention of the blonde woman in charge of the Target entrance. The woman looked like she might come over so Jade pushed herself off the wall and crossed over into the Mall, thinking how one of these days she should have a go at open-mike comedy, at the Rhino Room maybe. How hard could it be? Get people pissed enough and they'll laugh at anything.

There was still too much daylight left and Jade sat under an umbrella outside Maccas. Must be the day for weirdos, she thought, as a fairly well-dressed man began sorting, bare-handed, through the bins. At first she assumed he was looking for cans but then he pulled out a half-eaten Wendy's hotdog and after examining it carefully, shoved it in his mouth. *Oh, gross,* she thought. *As if anyone does that.* And right in front of everyone, as if they can't see. Still chewing the hotdog, the man fished a half-punnet of fries from the rubbish and pushed them in beside the dog, chewing with relish, his mouth wide open. Sickened, Jade moved away to cruise along the Mall. From further up she could hear the tuneless *plink plink* of the old guy with his xylophone. She often saw him there, sitting against a wall with his hat by his feet. His aimless tapping couldn't be called playing exactly but he had a busker's licence so couldn't be done for loitering. There was a story about him, a kind of urban myth that said he was a PhD in history, or biochemistry, depending on who was doing the telling. Anyway, he was supposed to have had some kind of breakdown and ended up drooling into his shirt, begging in the Mall. But really, she thought, who believes that?

Jade wandered down the little side street leading into DaCosta

Arcade and sat down with her back against the shady side wall of Harris Scarfe. She thought if it got any hotter her brain would melt. She smiled at the people coming and going through the Arcade, but they all seemed too hot and bothered to notice. Or maybe they were suspicious, she thought. Maybe just sitting there made her look like a bum. As an experiment, she tried the smiling standing up but still nobody paid her any attention. It was as if she didn't exist.

She noticed the boy while he was still in the arcade coming out of Venue-Tix. Tall and kind of lean, but muscled. Jeans faded from age instead of chemicals. Shaggy, dark-brown hair that he kept flicking out of his eyes. Eyes that grinned back at her when she smiled.

'How's it going?' she asked, when he came within earshot. He stopped, dropping his backpack on the ground in the way people do when they're going to hang around a while.

'Yeah, good. Fucking hot, but. Don't I remember you from somewhere?'

'Maybe. Dunno. Hey, you wouldn't have a spare fifty cents, would you?' She watched his eyes shift focus, sliding away from hers as he shook his head.

'No. Sorry,' he mumbled, shouldering his backpack.

'Oh, that's all right mate,' she said. 'I don't suppose you've got any food?'

Her words ricocheted off his back as he turned the corner into the Mall. It should be too hot to care what he thought, but still she wished she could take her words back, wished she hadn't asked him for money. If they'd kept talking he might have put her on to somewhere she could crash the night. *Who am I kidding*, she shouted aloud to the Harris Scarfe sign. She'd liked the look of him, that's all, and she knew what he thought about her.

Tributary, leading onto Rundle Mall

John De Laine

1.

Above our heads, a battered old network
of drainpipes.

Each dented inch a birdshit
Pollock.

Each brick in the wall
a tomb for Lenin.

Each shaving of paint from the skin
of a windowpane, a reminder of the rented room
that once was.

2.

Pass the bottle, friend,
and let me drink to Adelaide.
Pass the bottle, friend,
help me to love the streets.

Pass the time, my friend,
with me, in this lane, on this day.
Pass the time, my friend,
no one listens to what we say.

Pass me a blanket, thanks, good friend,
I need to sleep, to rest.
Pass me a blanket, thanks, good friend,
I tried my best, I tried my best.

RUNDLE MALL AND ME

Annette Willis

Early Morning Bruegel

Jude Aquilina

In Rundle Street: a grey-coated man pushes a trolley full of lumpy sacks from a dim alleyway, he grumbles at school kids who whistle and goad; a urine-stained doorway down the lane holds a sleeping man, newspaper-shielded from passing eyes; a clump of fluorescent cyclists flash by; a frenzied busker, missing a string, repels donors with his filthy feet and discord; twin toddlers in Shrek ears stare at an orange-vested, orange-bearded *Big Issue* vendor; a tall Sudanese teen wipes Hungry Jack's' window clean, stops to contemplate his reflection, and I wonder, as he might too, who is it that looks back at us and how did we come to be in this curious composition?

Passing Through

John Griffin

The two men carry ladders: Harry and Aldo.
Harry has two red buckets and a cloth.
Those who stand around have fox faces
hidden in planes of shade. Besides,
the day is warm in the Mall, the air
moves like sludge, and a random girl
is running her fingers across the threads
of the Gawler Place fountain. Harry
is slightly in front of Aldo, overweight
and walking fast. They do not notice
the shoppers and loungers, the busker,
the truant, the cop. None of us can see
the others, none of us would sense
the earthquake through the feet, a storm
of longing, or the shiver of the breath
of ghosts who walk there, sit, and stare.
Aldo and Harry are hurrying, almost there.

Outing

Anna Solding

Today, my mum killed my sister. Auntie Eddie, who isn't my auntie at all but one of Mum's old friends from school, came over to look after me. She's nice. Always gives me lollies and tells me not to say a thing to Mum. She can close one eye while the other stays open. Winking, she calls it. I can't do that. But I practise when Auntie Eddie comes around so that maybe one day I'll be able to wink back at her. That'd make her laugh. Like a pearly necklace, her laugh, she says. Mine's more like the rumble of a hungry tummy, I reckon.

She has two dogs. Doodle and Dag. They always come along when she takes care of me. Doodle isn't a poodle even if it sounds like it. No, she's a great big labrador and in the beginning I was a bit scared of her. Just a little bit, mind you. Now we're friends and she licks all over my face and stuff. Dag's old. She's a cross and Eddie don't even know where she came from, one day she just turned up limping and Eddie had to do the right thing. What the right thing is can vary but in this case the right thing means nursing Dag back to good health and letting her stay for as long as she wants. Eddie says she's had Dag for going on twelve years now and she's getting very old because she wasn't a puppy when Eddie found her.

Dag licks my feet and Eddie says:

'Let's go to the city.' She says: 'Let's not think too much today.'

'To break the boredom?' I ask, because that's what she usually says.

She looks at me with crumpled eyes and reaches out to touch my earlobe the way she sometimes does when she's distracted, but she's still staring straight at me.

'To calm the nerves,' she finally says, before reaching for the box of tissues on the kitchen sink.

I'm excited about going so I'm not sure how a trip would calm me down but I'm trying not to show it. I go to my room and start packing my small blue bag of favourite things that I might need when we're away. The shiny red marble with a chip like a fish taken out of it. Three books with silly pictures and stories that rhyme. Can't read 'em but I like the pictures heaps. Five Kinder Surprises. The secret hairband that I pinched from Mum's toilet bag. It smells of her. I like holding it close to my nose in the car because it stinks of wet dogs and old Macca's wrappers. The car stinks, not the hair band. Haven't told Auntie Eddie that, though. New Macca's wrappers smell good because I love Macca's. The cheeseburgers are better than at Hungry Jack's, no joke, like my half-brother says when he comes over sometimes. Mum never lets me have a whole Happy Meal, just the burger. She says we can't afford it. I should be happy with a burger and I am. Then we share a Coke.

Auntie Eddie buyed me a Happy Meal once. The special toy was a little soft cat. I still have it, hidden under my pillow. Mum says I'm too big to play with baby stuff like that. But I don't play with her. We talk, Juanita and me. I call her Juanita because I heard that name on telly one day and I really liked the actor lady who played her. She had big teeth and big hair. Mum has long, shiny hair and a gap to the side where one tooth was before it started hurting and she had to pull it out. It was all black and funny. Dark means dead, the dentist said. I wonder if my little sister's dark now. She couldn't be in the bin like the tooth, I know that. She'd be too big.

'Come on, Willie! Stop dragging yer feet, mate.'

Eddie straps me in. She doesn't have a car seat but she has a special cushion that I sit on so the belt doesn't cut my head off if we have an accident. She's never had one, in all her years of driving, she says.

'But it's better to be safe than silly, isn't it Will?'

I nod because I don't really mind the belt and I clutch my blue bag tight to my tummy as Eddie slowly backs out of the car port. We stop at red lights. Once, twice. The third time we have to stop Eddie whispers 'bloody hell' but I hear it anyway.

'Twenty cents.'

'Right.' She finds a coin on the floor and stretches back over to me without taking her eyes off the road. 'Thanks for reminding me.'

It's a gold coin and I wonder if I should tell her or if perhaps she knows and she wanted to give me a special one today. It's heavy and shiny. On one side it has 'roos and on the other a lady with a crown.

I sing a song from playschool but Eddie prefers the radio. 'Highway to Hell.' Dad plays that song heaps loud sometimes when Mum's at the shops and he's supposed to be mowing or something. I love my Dad but Mum says he's pretty useless, really. He likes eating nuts and throwing the shells in a bucket. I get to pick up the ones that fall on the ground, or if I'm lucky and he's in a beer mood I get to sip the stout and have a go at throwing. It always makes my stomach feel warm and funny.

'Turn it up, Auntie Eddie!'

'What's the magic word?'

'Pleeeeese.'

We slow down along the river. The pedal boats float like coloured paper.

'I wanna go on a boat.'

Eddie looks out the front window and doesn't say anything.

'We'll see,' she says after a long while. 'Maybe.' She points to a building sticking up above the trees. 'That's where Jackie is at.'

Jackie is Mum's name. But I call her Mum. Dad calls her Broad because of her country accent and because of her backside but I'm not supposed to mention that. Everybody else calls her Nugget because she is so small or maybe because she loves chicken nuggets more than anything else in this wide world. Except for me. She loves me the very most.

We park in the Myer car park and I get to press the button in the lift.

'I wanna see the pigs!'

Auntie Eddie nods but I can tell she's not really listening so I take her papery hand and pull her out to Rundle Mall. Outside is like when I brush my teeth in the bathroom after Mum's had a shower. My cap sticks and it's hard to breathe.

'This heat …' Eddie mumbles.

I don't mind it so much. Apparently, it's the hottest March ever but I reckon it's been nice. Just right, like Mum says when the sausages have been cooling on the bench for a few minutes. I like the heat because it makes Mum stay indoors to play with me in the lounge where there's air. It's a bit tricky for her to get up off the floor now that my sister's taking up so much space. Suppose that's all changed today.

Eddie touches my cheek. 'Let's not brood,' she says. 'You show me where those pigs are.'

'Right there, Auntie Eddie!' I point straight ahead to the one standing on his back legs searching for food in the bin.

Eddie chuckles. 'Aren't they cute?'

They look like they're made of gold. I know it's not gold but I can't remember what it's called. They have funny names like Augusta and Horatio. Eddie reads them out to me when I climb up to sit on one's nose. Or snout, as Eddie calls it. A couple of other kids stop to play too. It's a girl and her little sister. The girl's got long plaits with ugly pink ribbons and she's pulling her sister along even though she's obviously too small to climb.

'Wanna play?' I try and nudge her a bit but she pushes me away.

'Why'd I wanna play with you? You're dirty.'

She walks over to another pig, dragging her sister along behind her. The sister looks like one of those dolls you see in the toy shops. Chubby cheeks, curly hair and big blue eyes. She's the prettiest little thing I ever saw and all I can think about is that I'll never know what my sister looks like. I reach out to touch her cute face but the big sister pushes in between us.

'Don't touch her!'

My Dad has a short fuse and he says that sometimes I'm just like him. All I want to do is feel how soft her cheek is. The only thing stopping me from doing that is the witch with pink ribbons. She needs to go. I push her to the side. Not hard, just a small push but she stumbles and catches her foot in between Horatio's front legs and slams her head on his back before hitting the ground. The little sister stares at me with scared eyes.

'Sorry' I whisper to her. I didn't mean to scare the chubby face.

Now I can't reach out for her because Eddie is shaking me and screaming.

'What did you do, Tiger? Why is it always like this? Every time I take you somewhere you manage to fuck it up! We should have just stayed at home with the dogs.' She turns to the girls' mum who is holding the crying witch: 'I'm so sorry!'

I could explain that I just wanted to play, to touch a soft chubby cheek, that I never intended for the witch to fall, that it was a small push. But what's the point? They've all made up their minds about what happened. It's always my fault.

The witch is bawling her eyes out. When I cry like that Mum always says 'you couldn't even get a role in a B-grade movie, that's how unconvincing you are'.

People walk past going about their daily lives as if nothing has happened. As if my sister still exists. Or rather, as if she never existed.

There's sweat on my lip and I lick it off. It tastes salty and yummy and it helps me concentrate on not listening to Eddie's ranting. I pick at a sore spot next to my nail. Pulling the skin hurts really good.

The chubby cheeks stand hidden behind her mum, sucking her thumb and shuffling her feet. She's ready to leave, to move on to better things.

'… So now you go over there and tell her you're sorry.'

Eddie pulls me along by the arm and parks me right next to the girls.

'Sorry.'

I hear Eddie explaining to the mother that I'm going through a bit of a rough patch at the moment. The witch sticks her tongue out at me but I concentrate on pulling Augusta's gold tail rather than the girl's pink ribbon.

'Let's go!'

Eddie looks at me as if to say: 'Just you wait … I haven't quite fin-ished with you, young man,' the way Mum does, but all she says is: 'Yes, let's go.'

She takes my hand and we start walking. I wonder how the dogs are. If they have digged up the garden; if they're barking at the neighbour's cat, Silly (she likes teasing him, I've seen it before); if they miss us.

I know Eddie is annoyed with me from the way she walks, with big steps and no waiting.

'I want my mum!'

'I've told you, we'll pick her up on the way home.'

'When're we going home?'

Eddie drags me out of the sun, crouches down and holds my arms really tight. Too tight. She glares at me, as if she's all angry and sad at the same time.

'Will, my patience is wearing pretty thin here. Don't test it any more.'

She lets go of my arms which is a relief and then she hugs me instead which is a bit of a shock and slightly embarrassing just outside Harris Scarfe.

'I know that it's hard for you to understand but it's all for the best. Believe me.'

I nod and wiggle out of the awkward embrace.

'Can we go to the boats now?'

'No!' says Auntie Eddie with her angry voice but her eyes have little smiles in them. 'Haven't you got cheek to ask that …'

'Pleeeeese …'

She throws her hands up on the air. 'After all the trouble you've caused? You have to make it up to me. Be on your best behaviour when I get my shopping and we might go to the boats after.'

'I promise, I will.' I nod so hard I think my head will fall off.

'Let's go then.'

I trail her quietly through the Mall, stopping at an endless string of shops. At the lolly shop they have golf balls made of chocolate. They look yummy and I want to get one but I only have the gold coin Eddie gave me in the car and I left it in my blue bag. Now is not the time to ask Eddie for more. Have to be good. Wonder if Dad's done a hole-in-one today. When he goes playing after work he sometimes brings home presents from the course. Old golf balls and red, blue and even silver pegs. In the fake jewellery store there are pink ribbons just like the witch's. In the shoe shop Eddie tries on hundreds of shoes before my stomach starts rumbling.

'You hungry?'

'Mmmm.'

'Me too. How about Macca's? I just need to get one last thing and then we're done.'

She wants to buy a get-well card for Mum from the newsagent. I help her choose a pretty one with a big flower on it because I know Mum really likes flowers. I hope it'll make her happy.

'What would you like?' Eddie asks when we reach the front of the queue at Macca's. I don't want to push it because then I'll lose out on the boat so I just say 'whatever'.

'Cheeseburger? With fries?'

'That's great! Thanks Eddie.'

She laughs. Loud so that other people hear and they turn to look at us.

'You really are making an effort, aren't you? How about a Happy Meal?'

Now I smile too. Just a little bit because I have been good and I never asked for it, she offered so I can say 'yes' and have my second Happy Meal ever in my life. It is a juicy burger and the chips are crispy and salty just the way they should be. The toy is a silly plastic dog from a movie I haven't seen, but it doesn't even matter.

'Can we do the boats now?'

Eddie has that 'what should I do with you?' look that Mum has after I've played war in my room and the teddies have ganged up on the transformers, just before she gets the black garbage bag out.

'You sure you really want to? It's so hot …'

Yes. I nod. I have never been more sure.

'Right. Let's get it over and done with.'

It's a long walk but I don't complain. Eddie walks too fast. Sometimes I have to run to keep up.

'Look! There they are!'

'Hey Tiger Will! No running! There's cars here!' She holds on to my T-shirt when we cross the big road after the buses.

'I want a red one!'

Eddie comes panting after me down the hill to the river. She grumbles about the twelve dollar fee but I'm happy. We pedal hard together, to the water that shoots high in the air and all the way across to the other side.

There's something black floating in the water.

'What's that?' I ask Eddie and point to the blob in the water.

'A dead bird, sweetie. A swan.'

'How died it?'

Eddie looks at the bird again and shrugs. 'I don't know.'

My back is wet from pedalling hard and the sun hurts my eyes. Everything is bright and the boat's hot to touch. Eddie smells sweaty. The bird floats up and down on the waves.

'What happens when you die, Eddie?'

Eddie bites her lip. 'I wish I knew, Tiger. No one knows what happens.'

'Nana says you go to heaven.'

Eddie chuckles. She looks like she likes me again.

'Yeah, but your Nan is a fruitloop. You shouldn't listen to anything she says, you know that.'

The sun is burning my arms; I can almost see them turning pink. Suddenly I'm so tired I want to cry. I miss my mum and I want to go home.

'Hey, don't cry.'

She puts her arm around my shoulders.

'I'm sure your sister is happy wherever she is. You should be grateful, you know.' Her voice gets a bit shaky. 'Jackie did it all for you and your dad, so she'd still have time for you.'

I wonder if Mum did the right thing, just like Eddie did the right thing with Dag all those years ago.

The dead swan bumps into the boat again and again. I wipe my face with the back of my hand.

'Your sister had something very wrong inside. Here.' Eddie points to her stomach. 'Jackie would've had to be in hospital all the time.'

I sigh and nod. That's what they all say but I know she killed her. I know she couldn't cope with another child like me.

Eddie touches her eyes with her fingertips then looks at her watch.

'Should we go and pick her up?'

I look at the swan one last time before I start pedalling.

Boats for Hire

David Mortimer

The nervous boy and the doll-faced girl
Are out in a little cockleshell boat
They are maybe sixteen years old
And the boat spins like a pistachio shell

They are teaching each other to row

With two groups of friends
A boy-group by the water
And a girl-group up under the trees
Casting comments from dry land

And some exact tragedy elsewhere
Exercising no one's mind

Luckily it's Rymill Park
And the boy can get out mid-lake
And go for a walk in the water
And pull the boat to shore

Eight feelings towards, and away, from Adelaide

Rachel Hennessy

1.

This place is seeping into me, like a kind of grey sludge, the colour of the cement on North Terrace. It feels like it is filling me up and soon, too soon, I'll be stuck, permanently held here, like one of their monuments.

2.

The phone is ringing and today, day ten of a heat wave, I choose to ignore it. The tone of the ring is unusual – at least one of my friends has laughed at it, another one had jumped in fright (but Toni is always fragile, unable to deal with jarring) – and I hate the way the phone lights up, a beacon of demanding.

Even as I don't try to move, I know my legs are stuck to the leather couch. They do that now, in the heat, my sweat proving to be adhesive.

Underneath me, through the carpet, through the floorboards, in the space between the underside of the outside floor and the dirt ground, in that emptiness, I imagine it might be cool.

'It's too frickin' hot!' I yell.

The fan pushes dry air towards me, a sarcastic reply.

Under my childhood home, I remember, there'd been a dirt-lined basement (though we never called it that, it was always just 'under the house'), a storage space with the cobwebbed ends of brick pillars dotted around – the foundation of our lives – and there, always there, the world had been cool.

3.

I walk slowly down the leafy street, the wealthy street. It is too hot to walk fast.

Every house has a sign 'Bore Water In Use,' though I'd never heard any drilling. The signs are up to keep the water inspectors away, to reassure passers-by that the green lawns are perfectly legal. Through the high metal gates I try not to sneer openly at the sheer audacity of it: to dig deep enough into the ground, past all normal levels of existence, into your own private source of solace.

In one of the front gardens, an entire dodgem car fun-fair has been set up. A man in khaki pants and shirt is walking towards the gates where I stand, held by the dodgem cars. He holds a giant bunch of metallic balloons.

'All right for some, hey?' he calls.

Under the house, I remember, my father had once hidden a doll's house, building and painting it secretly for me on the weekends. As a cover story, he had told me it was for the next-door neighbour's daughter. The level of my envy back then still makes me blush today.

4.

I answer the phone.

'When are you coming back?' my mother asks (it could have been my sister, or my brother or even a friend, although most of those have given up by now; only relatives hold onto you longer than anyone else). I am used to the question.

I feel a rumble through the soles of my feet. The V8 cars are racing somewhere out there, gulping down the world's oil supply. I feel the relentless rhythm as they chase each other. I am too far away to really smell the petrol but it is out there, taking over the streets.

My childhood street, I remember, was a cul-de-sac, a loop where only resident cars would drive. On summer nights we would ride our bikes, chasing each other. Some driveways would be deemed 'home' and 'safe'. Others were to be avoided. Still others were no-man's land, neither scary nor safe, simply there.

'Soon,' I answer.

5.

I pass the road-works. An underpass is being hollowed out, the trucks beeping and reversing well into the night. They have closed off the main road, forcing the cars to take a longer route. Taxi drivers grumble whenever I say my address. When the underpass arrives, everything will be better, they assure me.

I like the fences, the quiet isolation of the walk across the parklands, dodging the magpie larks. Toni (the one who jumps at my strange ring tone) had made me promise never to walk across the parklands at night but I've broken that promise many times now. I laugh and tell her this isn't LA, the 'badlands' won't hurt me, but she is solemn and makes me renew my broken vow.

When I walked home every day from school, I remember, I passed through an underpass. My childhood friend would point out a new piece of graffiti – *If you notice this notice you'll notice this notice is not worth noticing* – and we would talk about the words we were going to write on the cement one day.

6.

I stroll along the riverbank, amazed that I have never seen this particular section – just before the dam, on the other side of the golf course – and spot a duck I have also never seen. A red speckle above its beak, fat and un-afraid, staring at me as I scrounge around for my mobile phone to take its picture. Something rare and unusual I hope.

Toni and her non-boyfriend try to identify it for me but it is in none of their – or my – bird books. We show the photo to whoever we know until someone bursts the bubble.

'It's a Muscovy duck,' the woman says, brutal and to the point. 'A whole heap of them were imported here and then culled, but I suppose some escaped.'

All the way from Russia, I think, although I have no real idea if the name is derivative.

I had spent one summer, I remember, accompanying my father to the beach with his metal detector, sure that we would find treasure. He waved the metal pad over line after line of sand and it was my job to keep track of where we had and hadn't searched. The sun would beat down and my head begin to ache but I held to the hope of finding something unique, only to be discovered in special places.

7.

On Kintore Avenue, I am escaping the tents of Writers' Week. It is hot again, ridiculous heat, where paper fans seem an insult. The heat is not enough to stop me, though, to eliminate the buzz, the thrill of all the words being spoken by the wisest of the wise. I have Greer's sass in my head, could kiss the ground on which I walk.

'Howdy,' a young drunk girl and her boyfriend make me move to the side of the pavement.

'Hey,' I answer quietly but the girl doesn't hear.

'Ignore me, will ya? Pretend I don't even exist hey?'

I stop walking and turn back to them. I don't want to be accused of this. The boyfriend is hanging back, clearly embarrassed by his high lover.

'I said "hey".'

The girl runs up to me and takes my arm. I continue to look her in the eye.

'Sorry, I didn't hear. You've got a quiet voice, you know?'

'Sure.'

'You have a good day, okay?'

She turns back.

One night when we'd been having fish'n'chips down at the local store – a rare event – I remember my father turning to a group of young men who'd been swearing loudly and asking them to please stop because there were children present. My sister and I had cringed but the men stopped, and apologised. 'There's a time and a place,' my father had said.

8.

I stand in front of the sandstone buildings of North Terrace, all of them are lit up, transformed from their traditional tan to pink and red and green, given three-dimensional patterns. A Festival piece that has proved so popular they've extended it. The state library is projected with books, the museum is crawling with spiders, the art gallery is painted with a mosaic. The Northern Lights have been localised and democratised.

A woman is pushing a pram toward me, not looking where she is going, pointing her child up to the spectacle. I step swiftly out of her way.

I am here. I should have written on the cement, if I'd been brave enough.

At Adelaide Writers' Week

Mary Manning

There's a poem blowing up
on the quiet grass near the rose garden.
It ripples petals over the woman in the shady hat,
and the baby dangling, strapped over her gauzy clothes.

Star-shaped plane leaves, veined like old hands
brush the baby's bare limbs.
His head is as neatly-furred as the trees' hanging seed-balls
which burst open in the heat and shower him with pollen.
He sneezes and beats his mother's breasts in delight.

The breeze puffs clove-scented smoke,
gently lifts the mother and child up above the trees
and over the West Tent,
then sighs them down behind the book-signing table

where the baby picks up a ballpoint pen
and writes his first beautiful couplet in an out-held book.

His mother wonders if he'll ever recover
from his first dose of poetry.
She'd rather he caught it later in life
when he'd built up antibodies.

Flight DJ 546 from Adelaide

Angela Smith

Because the supreme reality in life is fiction
It is vital not to meet the writer in person.
(*Notes Towards a Supreme Reality* by Paul Durcan)

Seat 22B wears blue:
spectacles, earplugs and polo top
with *KATE MORGAN*
WEIGHT LOSS CENTRE
picked out in pink on the pocket.
Shorts and shoes are blue too.
She is reading a magazine
open at page thirteen:
How to lose ten years.
I slump in 22C, reading Durcan.

I had stood in line
for Durcan to sign my copy
of *Greetings to Our Friends in Brazil.*
As he melted into his seat
in 39 degree Adelaide heat
he asked, 'Your name?'
'Just yours,' I replied, shying away
from the reality of the writer
and his mandatory familiarity
with the fawning Festival reader.

Take a Bow, Anthea Bell

Gillian Britton

There is urgent activity in the bowels of the Festival Theatre. It is the final night of Wagner's *Ring Cycle*; Brünnhilde has five hours of high drama ahead of her, culminating in her fiery descent into death, but here she is, a Norse god supporting her on either side, limping down the corridor toward her dressing room. Members of the cast, already kitted out in their black leather and hair extensions, their thigh-high boots and Alice Cooper makeup, line the walls in a macabre pageantry of sympathy.

The stage manager, Zoe, in mandatory black jeans and elastic-sided boots, walks behind Brünnhilde, talking into her head-set, barking the understudy into action, keeping the expletives to a minimum as she explains to somebody, probably the CEO, that Edwina Myer, their diva, their world-class trump-card Brünnhilde, had stepped backwards off her pedestal horsing about with Siegfried during the warm-up; had twisted or broken her ankle; was in no fit state to walk onto a stage, let alone sing arias for five hours and then be finally, apocalyptically immolated along with the entire infrastructure of the immortal realms.

Anthea Bell, on her way to the Green Room, hears all of this; she is caught up momentarily in the flurry. She skirts around Zoe, squeezes past a clutch of silvery Rhinemaidens and is suddenly level with Edwina Myer, who stares directly at her. She wills Edwina to remember her, but Edwina's eyes slide over her and away. Of course, it's hardly the moment; the woman's in pain, Anthea thinks. Still she wonders momentarily, before she flutters the thought away, if there is nothing left of who she once was for Edwina to recognise. As if she has sailed through her life leaving no visible trace.

She enters the Green Room, where gods and mortals in the full horror of their make-up mix democratically with the black-clad techies and orchestral members, drinking red wine and picking over plates of limp lasagne. There's animated discussion at one table about the day's play at Memorial Drive – India versus the Aussies. At another the harpist is giving a blow-by-blow of last night's *Sex and the City*. Further along, one of the Norns, made up to resemble tree bark, sprouting tendrils of fabric and rope, is breastfeeding a baby. Her husband sits by with the stroller and half an eye on a little boy who zooms in and out under the legs of tables and is suddenly face-to-face with the ghoulish Alberich, who has leaned down to collect a dropped fork. Alberich tinkles his fingers at the toddler and tries to smile warmly through his face paint but the toddler isn't buying it; he stands frozen and begins to scream and his father comes running to rescue him.

The understudy, Lesley Penhaligon, flies in, wrapped in a pink bathrobe, the first layer of her Brünnhilde make-up already applied, so that her eyes boggle out from a back-drop of white. She makes for the Norns' table, tells them the news about Edwina, then flies out again, kissing at the air, trilling a triumphant arpeggio.

All the while Anthea has been standing at the urn, waiting to make her cup of tea. She always has a cup of tea (tea and coffee are free) and a plate of vegetables before the performance. This is a matter of budgetary compliance (thanks to Barry's desertion she now has a mortgage again) and plain common sense: she likes to do her job well and wine would dull her reflexes. Not that it seems to hurt any of these people, she thinks. Once upon a time she wouldn't have thought twice about having a glass herself.

On a sudden impulse she abandons her styrofoam cup and walks to the servery. She orders a glass of red wine from the tall German woman with the bouffant hair, whom she suspects has an exotic history in no way involving hospitality; she pours Anthea's wine with a haughty, stiff-necked distraction, taking her money without so much as looking at her.

Anthea stands then, glass in hand, feeling suddenly exposed. It is not as if the possession of a glass of wine will change anything; she can't sit at any of these tables; after an entire season of complacent isolation it would be unprecedented and odd. She slips outside. She finds a tucked-away bench looking down the lawns to the rheumy Torrens. A near-empty Popeye drifts in to dock, dispatching a handful of elderly tourists, who are set upon by a recalcitrant black swan. She watches one old man chase it away with great whoops and flailing arms.

She laughs, and raises her glass to drink, but then she puts it down. She hasn't had a drink for months: with Barry gone, and the boys – Alex in Sydney, Matt in Thailand or Burma or somewhere – she feels too ... uninhabited. Drink would do nothing but slosh around in her empty spaces.

The last time she'd drunk wine, in fact, was when Barry and Loris had invited her for dinner in Loris's swanky city apartment. They'd cooked steak for her. Loris had made a salad full of hard little pome-granate seeds. No regrets, Barry had said; the boys were his pride and joy and he had Anthea to thank for that. He had raised his glass to Anthea. So had Loris.

'You are a fine mother,' he'd said, misty-eyed over his own mag-nanimity.

Wendy, her sister-in-law, tells her that this sudden disintegration of her life is an ideal opportunity to reclaim herself. Never too late, says Wendy, who, being twice-divorced, should know. They've been taking some classes together. Wacky sort of stuff, really, not Anthea's style, but it fills the time. There is a lot of time, suddenly, to fill. She's glad it is opera season.

And on that note, she gets up. Opera-goers are beginning to appear, women losing their heels to the aerated lawns; men, in the mid-afternoon heat, bloating like puffer fish inside their stiff collars. Emptying her wine into the bushes, trying not to think about the waste, she heads inside. She leaves her glass on the counter and moves back along the corridor, past the noise of the warm-up rooms, past the tuning harpist and a few nervous French horn players bleating out repeated dry runs of Siegfried's leitmotiv; over wires and boxed technology bearing scribbled signs – DO NOT TOUCH THIS BUTTON IF YOU IN ANY WAY VALUE YOUR LIFE.

She is at the stage entrance, a cavernous field of wood and gadgetry. Some of the orchestra are already down in the pit, whipping up and down Wagner's fast bits. She can see the hydraulic platform from which Brünnhilde earlier tumbled. She imagines stepping onto the stage, under the blaze of lights, but she is pushed aside by a sound technician on an urgent quest. He grips the backs of her arms and moves her to the right, as if she is a large, inexplicable urn.

She apologises and stumbles on, through another door to a reverse interior, and now she climbs, around and around in a spiral of stairs until she is stepping inside the perpendicular roof of the theatre, onto scaffolding, over air-conditioning tubes and wiring, to her door. She can hear the murmurings of the audience in the lobby directly beneath her. She can see their bright-lit crimson-carpeted world though the gaps around the light mountings. She hums a snatch of Wagner. If she sang loudly enough, she wonders, would they hear her down there?

But of course she doesn't sing. She flicks on the light, moves across the cramped booth to turn on computer, sound and overhead projector. She sits on her stool and puts her headphones on. Only then does she begin to cry. Part of her watches with a perplexed, motherly bemusement as her head drops onto the bench in front of her, sending her headphones awry, one earpiece clamping over her mouth and cheek while the other attaches to the loose knot of hair at the nape of her neck.

She tells people, if they ever ask, that she sits in the brains of the theatre, that these windows onto the stage and the auditorium are her eyes; that she has the vastest view of all from up here. What she doesn't say is that it smells – some mingled gaseous rankness – and that it is cold, as if excess refrigerated air is belched up from the auditorium. And that it is so far from anybody that if a fire raged through the place she'd be left to burn along with the rats and the boxes of outmoded technology that have been shoved up here in order to be forgotten. Out of sight, out of mind.

But this is ridiculous, she tells herself, this has to stop. She lifts her head, straightening her headphones, aware suddenly from the murmurings over the sound system that the audience are dribbling in and the orchestra are assembling, and the first surtitle, advertising sponsors, should be well and truly up.

In fact, she is at that moment paged by Zoe, 'Surtitles, are you up there? Where the hell is the sponsor slide?'

Oh yes, she thinks – they notice her when something's wrong. She picks up her red button and presses, and the surtitle appears above the stage: *The Ring Cycle is proudly sponsored by …*

The house lights go down. The audience settles. Zoe's voice booms through the theatre. 'Ladies and Gentlemen, we regret that Edwina Myer has suffered a minor injury this afternoon.' (Murmurs from the audience.) 'The role of Brünnhilde will be played this evening by Lesley Penhaligon.' (More murmurs – the disappointed variety – you don't pay a thousand bucks to see the understudy.) Poor Edwina, what bad luck, Anthea thinks – now there's something really worth snivelling about.

Onstage, the Norns appear and wail about the end of the world. Then the music burgeons and Brünnhilde and Siegfried, on their flower-studded pedestal, burst hydraulically out of the stage like a TV commercial for herbal shampoo, swooning all over each other, except that this is Lesley Penhaligon, not Edwina Myer. Edwina's Brünnhilde is sumptuous, fleshy, lusty, magnificent. Lesley Penhaligon's is very good – she's singing her fastidious lungs out – but she is not Edwina Myer and every person in the audience knows it.

Anthea sits on her stool, following the score, hitting her red button so that the English titles appear right in sync with the singers. She barely listens; she knows it by heart. At the moment it's all about undying love and heroic valour but it's pretty much downhill – treachery and murder – from here on.

She makes a decision during this first act. She won't sit up here during the interval like she usually does; she doesn't want to find herself weeping into her laptop again. So when the house lights come up she moves without hesitation, back down the fourteen loops of stairs and up the red carpet to Edwina Myer's door.

She knocks. She peers in. She might have expected a crowd but Edwina Myer is alone, slumped on a sofa with her foot up. She looks like a deflated hot-air balloon, half-costumed as she is. She holds a glass of red wine in her plump fist, breathing audibly from the large bellows of her lungs and staring at Anthea in the doorway.

'You won't remember me, of course,' Anthea says, laughing, she thinks, like a nervous horse. 'Anthea Bell, Queensland Conservatorium, class of 1984.'

'Ah,' Edwina Myer says, nodding obligingly. 'What was your instrument?'

'Voice, actually,' Anthea says.

'Ah,' Edwina Myer says, 'a singer. Anthea Bell. Oh …' A sudden memory lights her eyes, and she points a fleshy finger. 'You did the "Chants d'Auvergne" for the Young Performers – you won, didn't you, you little swine – you beat me. Yes, I do remember. Well, Anthea Bell, how are ya? It's been, what, twenty years? You've gotten skinny. Are you still singing? Pull up a pew – I could use some company.'

Offstage, Anthea remembers, Edwina Myer is as rough as a north Queenslander stepping off a prawn boat. She seats herself at the edge of an armchair, across from Edwina.

'No, I'm not singing,' she says, 'there was the problem …'

'Oh, Christ, it's coming back to me,' Edwina says, 'the botched operation on the vocal nodules, you poor sod – did you sue those bastards?'

'Well, no.'

'You should have sued the bloody bastards. What did you end up doing then?'

'Oh, I'm a behind-the-scenes person,' Anthea breezes, 'I'm the surtitler, among other things.'

'The surtitler? You mean a person does that? I thought it was computers.'

'The titles have to come in exactly with the singer, you see, which is different every time. Siegfried, for instance, came in three bars early at one point in the first act – he had to improvise a whole refrain over the top of an oboe solo.'

'Siegfried's inept,' Edwina says. 'The voice is a natural instrument, but he has no brain.'

'Things go wrong,' Anthea continues, 'you'd know that – people forget where they are, what they are supposed to be singing. I have to sort of smooth it over; make it look like it was supposed to happen that way.'

'Ah, the surtitler,' Edwina Myer says, 'invisible hero of the opera. Conduit between the artist and the uncomprehending masses.'

'Yes,' Anthea laughs. 'Yes, exactly. It's not the life I envisaged, but …'

'Well, what life is, Anthea, really?'

'But you've had marvellous success,' Anthea says, 'an international career …'

'Oh, yes,' Edwina says, 'it's a barrel of laughs. Remember this,' she says, pointing her finger again, 'off the stage, I'm just another obese woman with diabetes and gallstones. I walk down a street and people are disgusted by me. I stand on a stage, and I'm adored.' She tips her head back and laughs heartily at herself. 'Have a drink, Anthea,' she says. 'Why not?'

She shifts the heft of her body forward on the sofa, refills her own glass and another for Anthea, which she hands to her.

'To our sorry lives, eh, Anthea?' she says, 'and to this bloody ankle …'

Anthea gulps from her wine and seizes the moment. 'I think I might be able to help with that,' she says, 'I've been attending Reiki classes, you see. I'm a master. I could …' she hesitates, 'I could at least try and relieve your pain.'

Edwina Myer pumps out a laugh. 'Reiki, Anthea – you're an

alternative type? Oh, go on,' she says, nodding her head at the distended ankle, 'do your stuff – what have I got to lose?'

Anthea kneels on the floor and puts her hands on Edwina Myer's puffy ankle.

'Well, your hands are warm, at least,' Edwina says, and lies back, closing her eyes.

And so they sit for the duration of the interval. They talk. They reminisce. They drink. They compare failed marriages.

'But at least you had kids, Anthea. I was too selfish. Now I'm alone.'

'You're not alone.'

'I'm alone, Anthea, believe me. The lights go out, it's just me here.'

People poke their heads in from time to time, but Edwina shoos them away. 'I'm having treatment,' she says, 'from a master.'

'Did you ever sing again?' Edwina asks Anthea.

'No.'

'Why not?'

'Oh well, life …'

'But you wanted to, I can tell. Admit it, Anthea, you still want to.'

'Well …'

'You come over sometime before I leave and I'll give you some pointers. I can't believe they ruined you for good. Anyway, you're into this new-age stuff, aren't you supposed to be manifesting your own destiny or something?'

'I'm not really …'

'Fuck 'em, Anthea, that's what I say. Damned fool husbands and all the other idiots, fuck 'em all.'

Anthea runs back up the stairs for Act Two. She cues with marvellous accuracy. At the next break, she runs straight back down to Edwina.

'You witch,' Edwina says, 'What did you do to me? I'm feeling so much better.'

Zoe's voice trumpets through the blackness at the beginning of Act Three. 'Ladies and Gentlemen,' she says, 'Edwina Myer will return to the stage for the final act of tonight's performance.'

The audience cheers and applauds. Anthea beams, settling herself on her stool. She trills along with the Rhinemaidens, who loll about on the stage in their shimmery wet suits, trying to seduce Siegfried. Clueless Siegfried, who thinks himself a hero – who actually believes there are happier times ahead.

There aren't. Moments later he is dead, stabbed in the back. Anthea is so intent on watching she forgets a few cues and has to catch them up. Nobody notices, of course. Brünnhilde is doing her final aria; Anthea, almost without thinking, lifts her own voice and sings with her. *Siegfried I greet you in bliss* … the title reads. She finds herself standing, red button in hand, as Valhalla falls into ruins. The stage streams in walls of fire, the orchestra swells and flourishes and Brünnhilde, magnificent, walks into the flames.

The audience are on their feet, applauding with a deafening approval. Streamers and balloons descend from the ceiling as endless curtain calls are taken – for the singers, the maestro, the director, the orchestra, Zoe and the crew. But it is Edwina Myer that the audience screams for. Time after time she limps forward on the stage and bows before their hollering. Suddenly, straightening again, she raises her arms and quietens the audience.

'I have a particular thankyou tonight,' she says. She keeps her arms raised. 'To the invisible goddess of the opera,' she says.

The audience applaud good-humouredly, thinking she is making a feminist reference to the Almighty, but she hushes them with another motion of her arms.

'Anthea Bell,' she says. 'Can you see me up there? She squints into the stage lights, shading her eyes, looking up towards Anthea's window. The audience turn too, following Edwina's gaze, although the window is too high up for anyone to see.

'Take a bow, Anthea,' Edwina says.

And alone and invisible as she is, Anthea does. She bows deeply.

SENSE OF PLACE

Harvey Schiller

the grace

bernadette smith

Steven calls and is coming to visit. I say this is great but know he won't visit. My year in Adelaide has been filled with fortnightly calls from people saying they will visit but who don't. My mum did visit in February but that's different.

Steven is also the least likely to follow through as he has no money. Not having money is what defines him. No, what defines him is what he wears and his Lennon hair-cut and his fortunate-for-him Lennon nose. He can do, and often does, a great Liverpudlian accent.

I tell him this is great that you are visiting and to make sure he really knows I say whenever, just whenever, I'm still easy-going, the open-door policy has just moved across a state border. I have a sleeping bag and a chocolate-brown couch but no pillows.

Many a time back home I would awake to find Steven on the couch, asleep in leather jacket and tapered shoes. We had 24-hour cat access and this was Steven access also. I'd throw a blanket over him and turn the TV on quietly and only know he'd woken up by a snide but valid comment about some ad – no good-morning necessary. Once he'd gone to a mutual friend's back door in the night. Finding it locked and being too polite to knock, he had hip-and-shouldered it in. It was quite late and he probably didn't think that one through.

So it is with great surprise that the next Thursday night when *Neighbours* is on (I don't watch that of course, I am just wading in time between *The Simpsons* and *Futurama*), I receive a text saying Steven and girlfriend are just through the freeway tunnel; be there in ten.

I am delighted. I am tired. There's been a car accident involving seventy percent of the *Neighbours* cast; no one died. Mostly I am delighted. I am horrified that I'll be required to be drunk for a certain time. I am delighted that I'll be drunk before the *The Footy Show* is over.

We hug; his stiff, thin frame.

Jayne is from Essex.

Steven is defined by his serial monogamy, usually with English girls and now he's finally found one from close to the East End. She is lovely. She has distinct features, everything as deep or regular or full as required. She is tired from driving – Steven is license-less – and they took the coastal route from Melbourne too. We laugh about the place they call Keith. Good burgers but. No time is wasted and we go to the Arkaba. I know Steve will jump on the local brew idea so a slab of Southwark is eagerly procured. We say the name in the local dialect over and over.

The Bill is on. Steve loves *The Bill*. Jayne of course loves *The Bill*. I decide this is the only girlfriend of his I've ever liked. She isn't flippant; she has a flat back home. *West Wing* is on. I've never seen it and they kindly explain the key moments. I'm missing the *The Footy Show* because Steven takes his Victorian team information for granted. He is reading the *Advertiser*.

'This is worse than the *Herald Sun*' is his assessment by page five. State pride in tabloids. My cat enters the lounge, jumps on Jayne's lap. She expertly digs nails into his head.

They are a proper couple. They rehash on-the-road bickering. Steven was in charge of snacks on the trip. Under the pressure of adult responsibilities, he brought many packets of chips.

'I hate chips. They're rubbish. Crisps back home, now that's a chip,' Jayne says.

'Well you said, get anything.'

Steven ate three packets of chicken and three packets of BBQ chips from the Melbourne to Warrnambool stretch, along the Great Ocean Road. We used to call him The Seagull.

We don't drink many Southwarks. Jayne denies she is tired.

I am a terrible host. In the morning I am informed they will be going to the YHA. Steven had forgotten the 'no spare pillow' instruction. I have to work. I feel terribly Oskar Schindler about all things. They go to the zoo and to Port Adelaide and to Adelaide Oval, and we meet the next night at 5:30 at the Exeter because that is where one meets. Straight away, they gather and look through the street press. We talk about beer-glass sizes.

'So a pot …?'

'Is a schooner.'

'And a schooner …?'

'Is a pint.'

'Man, that's crazy. I'll tell you what else is crazy, the other day I met the guy who invented the half-flush.'

And so the conversation goes. We decide to formalise the inevitable pub crawl in a linear fashion so back-track to the start of the line, The Stag, where our glass-size discussion is further confused with its faux-Britannica pint-pints. It would have been better if they never existed here at all and locals couldn't even conceptualise them as glasses, like the Indians who can't see the ships on the horizon.

'So when did you guys meet?'

'Three months ago.'

'I thought it was heaps longer,' I say, and quickly realise I'm confusing Jayne with the previous English girlfriend. I cover.

'It's just that you guys seem so … couple-like.'

'We've only spent one night apart since we met.'

This is what Steven was after: this is what Paul and Linda McCartney said after their one-hundred years of marriage.

They tell me about when they met. It was – of course – at St Jerome's, and Jayne was at the bar, wearing an Iggy Pop T-shirt.

'So I was like: *Right, here we go hey.* And so I said …'

'He was staring at my chest and said *Iggy Pop hey?* He was mangled.'

'And so I said *A Brit hey? You aren't from the East End are you? You know what they say about girls from the East End?* And then later you were kissing that jerk outside.'

'Yeah but I went home with you.'

They've told this story before; they still can't believe their luck. Jayne's visa is running out soon and Steve is going to join her over there at the end of the year.

I want to show them the Adelaide bits that are closest to the Melbourne bits we love. So, just like in Melbourne, we walk west.

'North Adelaide, is that like North Melbourne?' Steve asks.

'No, it's more like Carlton, if Carlton was settled by Germans not Italians. Sorry I couldn't show you the sites today.'

'No, this is what I wanted to see. You can see dolphins or coast or vineyards anywhere. I wanted to see Friday-night Adelaide. It's the only capital I haven't been to before.'

'What, you've been to Brisbane?'

'Yup.'

'Perth?'

'Yup.'

'Not Darwin?'

'What is this? *The Goon Show?* Yes.'

Jayne is wearing those little ballet slippers that have infested women everywhere. And I'm not sure if it's them, or the little feet they contain, but she walks slowly as Steve and I talk on ahead. Or maybe it's intentional, her slipping behind. Maybe they've had a fight and I'm in the way, without the social skills to pick up on such festerings. What to talk about that is neutral, inclusive; such conversations don't exist except in French New Wave cinema. I point out King William Street as we pass it: now they are about to see Adelaide.

And I think he'll never make it to the East End at the end of the year. And Jayne is aware of this and defensive, or, spending 89 out of the last 90 nights with him means it may not be galactically disastrous were he not to make it. She is playing the Modern Woman role: you don't just move countries for a relationship; the economic rationalisation of love.

It is at the World's End when things go wrong. If not wrong, then at least comes the realisation that this may not be a perfect night like nights of old. And if things are going to go wrong they should go wrong at a place like The Stag, not here.

We get a table outside. People around us are lethargic on plastic chairs. Jayne has gone to water. Steven wants to talk about our things; he leans to me as he speaks. I can't see her face for his sharp shoulder.

'Remember at Stewart Street with the bed? Carrying all the planks. I wish I still had that bed.'

This is good. Now I can explain the story to Jayne with much mirth.

'So, what happened was, Steve had just moved in. Actually, that's a funny story too about when he moved in. In his interview he read this poetry about this girl …'

Shit.

'Poetry hey? You never wrote poetry about me,' Jayne says. But her voice is teasing.

'But that's because we never spend time apart. There's no need.'

Good save.

'Anyway, back to the bed …'

Shit. The bed story is about us building a double bed for him out of milk cartons and planks we'd found in the car park next door, a double bed that he needed as a girl was coming to stay with him.

'Hey, what's with all the queuing for buses?' Steve asks.

'I don't know. I haven't figured that one out yet.'

'What happens if you don't queue?'

'Don't know. Never tried it. I don't think anyone has. You should see the bus drivers here though. They're all your favourite uncle, just delighting in driving you to where you want to go.'

We ponder. Jayne's momentary revival minutes ago has not re-appeared. And Steve is dropping off too.

'Ah …'

Here we go; he's got something good.

'– remember the fight, with Wayne …'

'I wasn't there, but of course I remember. It went all kung-fu or something didn't it?'

'Yeah, the other guys just started giving me a hard time for nothing, about my clothes or something, and Wayne – remember he was in tough-guy phase then – he went nuts, took off his belt.'

'That's right, post-Glasgow Wayne.'

Steve is laughing hard. Whenever he laughs, and it is often, it's always hard; his face breaks. But Jayne just yawns. And I don't know how it happened or when, but here is what she is saying.

'That's when I got sick of backpacking; all anyone wants to do is drink. They go see one temple or something, then to the ex-pat bar. No one bothers trying to actually see the country, meet locals.'

She is talking about backpacking Indochina but what she means is us. She means her holiday with Steven to Adelaide where she wanted to do all this stuff and yet here they are, at the World's End.

Somehow in our stilted conversation the Kava Hut comes up. I'd told Steve about it before.

'Is it close?'

'It's just up there.'

'Should we go?'

I look at Jayne; she is neutral.

'We could,' I say. 'But it's getting late. I mean, I'm okay, but maybe you guys want to get going?'

Steve looks at me as though I have said I've never heard of the Beatles and what a stupid name for a band anyway.

'It's 9 o'clock.'

'Well, yeah. Jayne?'

'Kava Hut? Sure. Especially if it's close. My feet are killing me.

These stupid fucking shoes. I'm going to throw them out.'

She is martyring herself.

I'd explained to them about kava and that it is very difficult to pin-point an effect, even if you buy take-away and make the strongest kava ever made. But I liked it.

We look at the menu on the door. *Kava, Wormwood, Skullcap.*

'So, we'll just get regular?'

'Regular? Why don't we get the super?' This is Jayne. I didn't expect this from Jayne.

Jayne goes up to the bar.

'Three supers please.'

They must have many Kava Huts in Essex.

The woman makes our kavas. We all chat about kava, about Fiji and legalities. This woman makes you feel like you are entering her house and she is so glad you have visited. Relax, take your shoes off.

Three coconut shells, sliced oranges. Jayne carries the tray out the back, through the deep sand, past the uni-sex toilets. It's all tropical-themed out the back: plastic palms in the corners, Rio lights.

We sit on the benches. Our eyes are brighter from the lights.

'Cheers! Ah shit, this tastes shit.'

'You get used to it. Eat some orange.'

Within say, 45 seconds, there has been a transformation. So it can't be the kava, it's just the kava-ambience perhaps. Or maybe it's nothing, just time. Maybe nothing was wrong with anyone and now that we are old not every moment has to be supersonic.

We sit and drink, some photos are taken. Three-way talk. Now we are sentimental.

'Jayne said,' Steve says, '*I got some free days, let's take a holiday before I go.*'

'So Steve says *Let's go see Bern because I have to see her before I go.*'

'And Jayne says she has to meet you and so here we are.'

There may have been some hugging and telling to Jayne that she was my favourite of Steve's girlfriends.

Our shells empty.

We have a finishing pot at the Grace on the way to the YHA, surrounded by the sound bricks of the courtyard walls.

'Isn't it?' I say, a beaming tour guide.

'Oh, absolutely,' they both say.

Insomniac Rhapsody near Gilbert Street

Jill Jones

You sleep in a little cage,
see the slats and the bindings
of moonlight,
the glare of the Optus building.
Today another beer can
appeared on a sill,
cars stop by for moments.
It's a characteristic of trade:
if you need the money
you need to relax and swallow.
It all ends up like an empty container
while the chains and the cherry picker
rattle morning, far too early
after the deal over the road,
the dog barking in the clinic
car park.

Who says nothing happens here?
Each day mail is readdressed
and the police helicopter lifts
towards the hills.
On the radio farmers bless the rain.
Gouts of it drench the bitumen.
Another second is idling.
It's still months before the dust.
Somewhere – snow.

Something's melting in your brain.
Another dream
orgiastic as your old city
taking up the coast,
whose desalination
threatens your pH balance.
What runs through you will get you.
Sleep is only trash
you can't escape.

Guarding the Pageant

Stephen Orr

I saw my future in the budgie's beak. It was the Earth Fair, and you could have your fortune told by a small, yellow bird – one revelation for three dollars, two for five. Of course, I just laughed it off but my daughter, a clever, anti-*Pony Club* sort of kid, urged me to have a go.

So I paid my money and sat on a stool in front of the cage, and a short, wiry-haired old girl said, 'Go on, talk to him.'

'Talk to him?' I asked.

'He has to know something about you.'

So I told the bird my name (Sam 'Mad Dog' Morgan), address (... Avenue, Wynn Vale) and place of employment (Salesian College); I told him about my son, daughter and wife. And then the old girl said, 'Now, tell him something about *you*.'

'Me?'

'Yes,' she smiled.

I stopped to think. 'Well,' I began, hesitantly, 'some people think I'm a bit of a comedian.'

'Go on,' she beamed.

'I've written a few comedy skits, and sent them to Channel Nine,' I explained, wondering why I was sitting in the middle of a school oval sharing my innermost thoughts with a budgie.

'Tell the budgie about the narcolepsy meeting,' my tall, buck-toothed, brown-eyed son grinned.

'Yes,' I smiled. 'You see, it's the Narcolepsy Association's AGM, and one by one they fall asleep, until the camera shows the whole table, with everyone snoring.'

By now there was a queue of people waiting. The old girl said, 'That should be enough,' and produced a seed tray, half-filled with budgie food and half with little folded notes. She opened a door on the cage and placed the tray inside. The hungry bird started picking at the seed, swallowing a few grains before picking up a piece of paper. After he'd dropped it the old girl slid her hand into the cage and retrieved it – opening it up, looking at me, smiling and saying, 'Lucas knows.'

'Lucas?'

'He says, "Follow the Way of Truth, It leads to Happiness".'

I looked at her. 'What does he mean … God?'

'Not necessarily. Truth.'

My son Liam was pulling on my sleeve. 'Come on, Dad, you said we could do the three-legged race.'

Well, the Earth Fair was eighteen months ago, and a lot of things have changed since then. If I was having my fortune told today I'd have to tell the budgie the following – Name: Sam Morgan; Address: living alone in a one-bedroom flat in Salisbury Downs; Place of employment: various – working as a guard for Four Squares Security; Relationships: separated from wife of sixteen years (Avril), nine-year-old daughter (Sarah) and eleven-year-old son (Liam).

Yes, a lot can change in eighteen months. From a thirty-five square home at Wynn Vale to a flat; from teaching at Salesian College to a security guard (which isn't all that different, I suppose). From freshly ironed clothes to used shirts doused in deodorant to make them wearable; from teaching physics to guarding pageant floats on Adelaide's South Terrace – and all because of that budgie (perhaps).

The story I'd like to tell took place last night, on the eve of the city's annual Christmas pageant, as six other guards and I made sure that no one tampered with the floats. Since there are so many floats, and since there's not enough time on Saturday morning to drive them all over from the Richmond warehouse, they're ferried over by a small army of drivers the night before. They're parked in a line that concertinas two times before moving to the next stretch of road and doubling up again. This way about two hundred floats can be parked along a seven-hundred-metre stretch of city road.

And there they sit, through the night, waiting for their big moment – waiting for the thousands of Credit Union employees to arrive at sunrise on Saturday morning; waiting for them to pull on their fluorescent clown wigs and oversized novelty boots; waiting for them to apply their make-up and practice riding their thirty-centimetre high bikes; waiting for the marching bands to arrive and find their place between the floats; waiting for the fairies to start sprinkling tinsel, the fiddlers to fiddle, the tellers-dressed-as-farmers to harness their motorised sheep and for Father Christmas to gather his sack of toys (as all the kids think, *Has he got enough for everyone?*) and settle into his sleigh.

As jobs go, this is a good one. At least there's something to look at. I'd just spent the last month standing outside the Klemzig branch of the National Bank. We're told we can't be on the phone, listen to our mp3s or even make conversation with customers. No, we're there to work, ie, to stand and look menacing. Yes, we can walk around (within a two-metre radius of the entrance), have a drink and even eat our lunch, but if we read anything (even a gas bill) we could face instant dismissal. We're meant to have our eyes open and watch for trouble. This is the sort of job I warned my students they'd end up with if they didn't study. Last week one of my old Year 12s walked past, but I pretended to cough, and turned away.

Guarding the pageant is a very important job. What if, for instance, some little hooligan came along with a screwdriver and punched holes in the float's tyres? There'd be no pageant. Hundreds of thousands of people would have to be told to stay home, but many would already be in the city, and imagine their anger, and how congested the trams and buses would be, and all of the crying children?

Our group of guards met at six o' clock outside the Green Dragon Hotel. We were given some rather curt instructions. 'No one, repeat, no one, can come within three metres of the floats. They can look, they can take photos, but hands off, folks.'

I started my night beside the pirate float – a twelve-foot high fibreglass Bluebeard growling at the crowd, his broom bristle mo fluttering in the breeze as birds sat on his cap and relieved themselves. Then there was a scrawny pirate using an old bottle as a telescope and a huge two-tonne pirate looking at where the crowd would be with amazement as he guarded a treasure chest full of coins, necklaces and crowns.

I looked at the pirates and smiled. Cute. I knocked on Bluebeard's boot and it sounded hard and hollow. The pageant could transform flesh into fantasy. Just then I remembered sitting behind the blue line with Sarah and Liam two – maybe three – years before, watching this same float drive past. I remembered the smoke coming from Bluebeard's ears and the pre-recorded growls and pirate-speak coming over an old, tinny-sounding PA. I remembered the clerks-as-pirates running beside the float, threatening the onlookers with cardboard swords and hook-hands. And I remembered Liam looking up at me and saying, 'This is the best one yet,' as he smiled so hard I thought his cheeks would pop. And then, perhaps, my eyes frosted over, and I had to wipe them, pretending it was hay fever instead of happiness.

And I wished the pageant would last forever.

But it didn't, and doesn't. I can also remember Avril staring at a mother and father who'd sat their kids in front of Sarah and Liam. Yes, Avril had spoken up, as usual, saying, 'I believe our children had the front spot,' as I said, 'Don't worry, they can share.' But she wasn't having any of that.

'Typical eastern suburbs attitude,' she mumbled, and the other mother said, 'Pardon?'

'You heard me. Today's meant to be about the *kids*,' who by now had all moved to accommodate each other.

I paraded up and down my stretch of South Terrace, passing Nellie the part-fibreglass, part-fabric, part-steel elephant who, as I remembered, was accompanied along Grenfell and Currie streets by a group of loans officers bathed in fake tans. They wore glaring blue, yellow and red velvet jackets, three-quarter pants and sandals and carried bamboo canes to tap the heaving, diesel-driven beast on the rump. I wondered what these people must have thought when they saw a real Asian in the crowd, and who was most embarrassed.

Darkness settled across the grammar school on one side of the terrace and the parklands on the other. Yellow lights on stobie poles blinked to life, and it was officially night. A few families with excited, expectant kids strolled along the terrace – dads looking at me as if to say, *What if you turned your back for a few minutes …?* Just after nine o' clock a group on a buck's night emerged from the Green Dragon and one, a short, stocky kid with shaving cuts and a high voice, jumped the cordon and grabbed Nellie's horsehair tail. 'She won't shit on me?' he asked me, as the others laughed.

I just shrugged, remembering my buck's night, what seemed like a lifetime ago. I was so excited to be marrying Avril, to be leaving home and starting a new life. I wondered what the budgie would've told me back then. 'Don't do it. Just don't do it.'

I strolled up and down South Terrace, past floats that reminded me of other times, other places: the Seven Dwarfs, the Timber Cutters, the *Anything Goes* cruise ship and the black, white and grey *Maltese Falcon* float. Wood, fibreglass, steel and paint provided nugget-sized bites of fantasy, worlds beyond acceleration coefficients and broken line-trimmers, wildly fictional orthodontist's bills and staff meetings that run past six; beyond Steve Martin-style happy marriages and *Neighbours*-like communities. Ali Barbar instead of algorithms. Tom Sawyer instead of tax returns.

Frank, a twenty-year Four Square veteran, brought me a coffee and we sat on the Toyland float to rest our legs.

'Nice job?' he asked, with a guttural, Godfather voice.

'Different,' I replied.

'Someone said you were a teacher.'

'I was.'

'So what are you doing here?'

I stopped to think, and smile. 'I quit my job,' I replied.

'Why?'

'To annoy my wife.'

And then he smiled. 'Serious?'

'Serious … sort of. There was more to it … We didn't get along, and she didn't appreciate the sacrifices I was making, so …'

I stopped, realising I hardly knew him. He slapped me on the shoulder, slurped his coffee and wiped his mouth on his forearm. 'Women can be bitches,' he whispered, as though one of his two ex-wives might hear. 'They get their claws in, you know what I mean?'

'I know.'

'You did the right thing.' Then he stopped to think, looking into the sky and tilting his head. 'Bet you miss the money though?'

I looked at him and shrugged. 'What's to miss?'

'You got another girl yet?'

'I don't want another girl.'

'I got a cousin …'

'I could imagine.'

'If you just want sex …'

'Thanks anyway.'

A few minutes later he set off to check on the other guards, and I continued my stroll. It must have been after ten when a mother and father with a six- or seven-year-old daughter wandered past the Toyland float. The girl couldn't believe her eyes – hundreds of presents, some of them as big as washing machines, piled up at the base of a five-metre high Christmas tree. She darted away from them, slipped under the cordon and climbed onto the float. 'Get off,' her mother called.

The girl ignored her. She crawled towards the pile of presents, grabbed one and discovered it was stuck to the float. She pulled at it but it wouldn't budge. Then she looked at her parents and scowled. Her father started laughing but her mother kept repeating, 'Get down, this instant.'

I watched from behind a hedge as the girl's scowl turned to a smile, and she started trying to lift the other presents.

'This instant,' the mother barked.

The girl looked like Sarah – mousy-blonde hair, a button nose dissecting a pair of demonic eyes, large, strong piano hands and a will that couldn't be tempered by reason. Sarah, on every Christmas morning of her life, sorting through presents like a small tsunami, ripping, examining plastic-wrapped dolls and games and exploding with joy, throwing herself on me with open arms and saying, 'Thank you, Daddy,' between kisses, although it was generally Avril who'd bought the presents.

If she found one of Liam's presents she'd roll it to him across the carpet or just brush it aside or say, 'Liam, that's the basketball you asked for.'

Eventually the girl crawled back to the edge of the float and the father helped her down. She crossed her arms, stamped her feet on the road and said, 'They're not real.'

'What did you expect?' the mother replied, turning and walking on.

I watched as the girl smiled knowingly at her father, taking him by the hand and lifting the yellow rope for him to walk under. She saw me and for an instant looked guilty, but then just raised her eyebrows as if to say, *So, what are you gonna do about it?*

I smiled and the father winked at me, and I wondered if Sarah was home asleep or reading or watching TV. I felt, as I did thirty times a day, that I'd made the wrong decision by putting myself first, especially when it seemed like every other parent on the planet was doing the right thing.

But then I looked at the mother and remembered a warm March afternoon last year, when I walked in the front door and found Avril on the phone. I put down my bag, smiled at her, and waited until she was finished. Then I said, 'Guess what?'

'What?'

'I quit.'

She smiled at me as she stirred something on the stove. 'Quit what?'

'Work.'

'One day,' she continued smiling.

'No, today,' I repeated. 'I quit.'

And then it dawned on her. She took the time to turn off the stove, look into a sink full of dirty dishes and say, 'You didn't?'

'I did.'

Then the fireworks began. 'Why?' she asked, and I just shrugged and said, 'Because I don't enjoy it any more.' Then she asked about the mortgage, school fees and bills and I reminded her that we had enough savings for a year or so.

'While you do what?' she asked.

'Write this novel I've been planning for the last eight years.'

'Are you stupid?'

'And after that I'll get another job. There's plenty of work for physics teachers.'

'But you didn't even ask me.'

'I did, for the last five years, and you always said, "One day, when the kids have finished school".' And then I looked her in the eyes and whispered, 'I could be dead by then.'

'We all could.'

'That's the thing, isn't it, you couldn't give a rat's arse.'

'I supported you for years.'

'So what?' I stopped, glaring at her. 'So, so now we'll make it work. I'll get my book written and you – '

'Ring up the principal. Talk to him. It's not too late.'

But I just smiled.

And that was the beginning of the end. She kept pleading for another few days, and I kept ignoring her, locking myself in my study and reading about Daisy Bates for the Great Australian Novel I was going to write. And then she tried a different approach – ignoring me, talking to me through the kids and refusing to acknowledge my presence in the house. After two days of this I said to her, 'Come on, grow up, it's not such a big deal – twelve months.'

'You didn't even ask me,' she blurted.

'I did.'

'You only think of one person.'

'Bullshit. I've spent years thinking of everyone else.'

'You could've asked for leave.'

I stared at her and everything I'd been thinking for the past few years crystallised – small compromises leading to bigger ones. She'd started off choosing my shirts, then hobbies, cars, houses and finally dreams (sounds corny, I agree, but how else could I say it?). The words of the budgie were sounding in my ear.

'What do you think of me?' I asked.

She didn't reply, and it was then I knew. I couldn't remember when I'd ever loved her, or how, or for how long. She'd become a sort of assembly-line foreman, telling me how to put my life together, inspecting the finished product and putting a defective sticker on it.

In a fit of rage and revelation I went to our bedroom, took a case from the robe and started packing. She followed me in and stood staring, smiling, her arms crossed. 'Nice performance.'

To be honest, I think I was mainly bluffing at that point. 'You think I won't?'

'Gonna tell your kids where you're going?'

I stared at her, and decided.

Twelve months. Daisy Bates would get written. I'd get to rediscover the 'Mad Dog' in Sam Morgan and she'd be brought back down to earth.

At least that's how I remember it happening. Then there were the three nights in a motel, the flat, the lawyers and money taken out of my account – and then Four Squares, the National Bank and the Christmas Pageant.

And Daisy Bates went unwritten.

I moved down to the Barn Dance float. There was a small barn made of planks of red, blue, pink and purple wood. The loft was filled with fresh hay that smelt Kadina-early-morning – paddocks full of sheep nibbling stubble, hungry pigs grunting and someone starting a giant header and tuning its radio to talkback. An area had been left in front of the barn for cowgirls to prance around old milk pails, lanterns, wagon-wheels and a Hills Hoist with a thousand corks blowing in the doughnut-scented breeze. I could just hear the music and see the dresses flying in the air; I could see the straw hats and ryegrass hanging from the corners of mouths. Maybe even a Shetland pony or a lamb from the district manager's hobby farm at Gawler.

It was still, and mostly quiet, except for the hum of a distant air-compressor. I pissed in a bed of red and white petunias and returned to sit on the Barn Dance float. Someone had painted a line of horses, nose-to-tail, along the bottom of the sides of the barn. They were simple two-tone horses without mouths or ears and their eyes were a single white dot of watery paint that had run, leaving them crying milk-white tears.

Liam was the artist in our household. I'd given him money to buy canvases and a set of oil paints and he'd painted aliens landing in our backyard, Jackson Pollock-inspired forest scenes, portraits of Avril and Sarah and one of me filling a blackboard with nonsensical physics formulae.

I touched one of the horse's white eyes and the paint flaked and fell off, and I suppose he was blind after that.

'What do you think of this one?' Liam asked me, as he sat in the corner of the living room of my flat the previous Sunday.

'What is it?' I asked.

'The budgie, remember, at the fair?'

'I remember,' I smiled. It was a Picasso budgie – fat, misshaped, its yellow body striped with pink and purple paint. The note in its beak had grown to the size of a large encyclopaedia and I wondered if it wasn't the budgie (or Liam) telling me that life is far more complex than a fortune cookie message.

I sat on the floor beside my son and asked, 'What's written on the note?'

He smiled at me. 'I couldn't remember.'

But I could – 'Follow the Way of Truth, It leads to Happiness'. Or this, sitting in a hot flat that smelt of cooking oil and petrol, its torn shagpile full of dust mites and dirt, the sun beating on the cracked window as the air-conditioner made enough noise to drown out the telly without actually cooling the room.

The Truth? Happiness? Ha!

'That's a damn fine budgie,' I said. 'But I think he was wrong.'

Liam looked confused. 'How?'

I just smiled and put my arm around his shoulder. 'I'm sorry,' I whispered, without thinking.

'Why?'

'Because of … all this.'

He shrugged. 'Mum says you'll get over it, when you're finished with Daisy.'

I touched the tip of his nose, and almost laughed. 'She does, eh?'

'Who's Daisy?'

'Daisy, that's what the message said,' I explained.

'What?'

And then I pointed to the painting. 'I didn't know budgies had teeth.'

It was almost five-thirty when the horizon started to lighten from black to purple, to a blue that promised day between the rooftops of south Adelaide. I sat yawning, rubbing my eyes, beside the Jolly Swagman – a five-metre-high sheep rustler who had slept the night (and his whole existence) beside a cellophane river, waiting for a giant Murray Cod to pull on his string fishing-line. He wore patched jeans that were held up by a length of twine; his toes dangled in the river and his nails, smelling of fresh paint, were clogged with real dirt and lint.

I took an envelope from my top pocket, opened it and produced a pile of colour photos. The first showed Sarah and Liam playing under our nectarine tree. I looked at them both – tall, lanky, brown-skinned – and decided I'd make a phone call when I knocked off. If I drove straight to Wynn Vale, picked them up and returned to the city I'd be back in time for the pageant. I could find a nice spot on the southern end of King William Street and settle in with my kids.

That way I could reclaim the pageant. Our pageant – fantasy

made flesh. I could tell them, 'I almost fell asleep on that float,' and they could think, 'so what?'

The next photo showed the kids eating spaghetti, their faces covered in pasta sauce. Avril stood beside them, trying to wipe their faces with a flannel, as I (I suppose) just stood laughing, reaching for my camera and telling Avril to let them go.

Avril – growling at the world at the front of her own Bluebeard float, forming fibreglass skin, donning an eye-patch and shaking her hook at the world. Which made me the Jolly Swagman, my felt hat down over my eyes as I snored, waiting for a fish that would never take the bait.

But that's life, I guess. You make your own happiness, or misery.

Christ, I thought. *That's* what the budgie meant.

I looked at Avril's mean eyes and decided I didn't need her any more. I took the spaghetti photo and threw it in the bin beside the float.

I could hear her picking up the phone when I rang.

'Hi.'

'Are the kids doing anything this morning?'

'Sarah's got netball.'

'Ah …' A long pause, as I took a deep breath. 'I was gonna take them to the pageant.'

Then I could hear her thinking, the little clogs in her mind intermeshing.

'Hold on, I'll ask them.'

But then she stopped to think again.

'How's Daisy going?' she asked.

'Still in the desert with the black fellas.'

'Like you?'

'Me? I'm a black fella, eh?'

'… hold on.'

So I reached into the bin, retrieved the photo and put it on the bottom of the pile. I couldn't edit her out of my life, or back in, yet, perhaps. But photos are good like that – they compress time, showing you what's happened, what's happening, and perhaps what's to come. Flesh and fantasy in a snapshot.

I looked up and a hippo was staring at me. The float was called 'Hippo's Hot' and it consisted of a giant purple hippopotamus sitting in a cooking pot. I assumed that very soon the natives would arrive to paint their bodies, don their grass skirts and gather their spears. Then they could tend the fire under the pot as Hippo, thinking they were giving him a bath, continued cleaning himself with a scrubbing brush, sponging his red-hot face, popping the bubbles and laughing as though this was the best day of his life.

And perhaps it was.

The next photo showed the kids again, and Avril, but this time she was laughing along with them at Molly, our ex-dog, dressed up in Liam's old Spiderman costume.

And then I heard singing, and looked up to see an old man dressed in a holy track suit and cardigan, sitting in Father Christmas's seat on the Santa float. He'd climbed the ladder left there for the real Santa. He sang and then took a swig from a bottle in a brown paper bag. '*The First Noel …*'

As claret dribbled down his dirty, grey beard.

'… *the angels did say … sing …* Fuck, I don't know.'

And for a moment my future stretched out the entire length of King William Street.

At *The Flash*, before work, November morning

Ken Bolton

A Russian woman in my shop
begins to talk, & finds she cannot stop
'They wouldn't know *Apollinaire*
from an *aperitif*,' she despairs …
her fellow students. An
architect-trained
interior designer, from St Petersburg—
thirty-something,
soft, Georgian, Marie Laurencin sort of
face. It's true, I don't sell Apollinaire much—
& might be the only place to stock him,
here, Adelaide, Australia. Australia
may have turned out
a wrong move.
Her friends at home
              'are doing okay'—
& talking about Apollinaire, maybe.
Maybe not. I wonder where they do
talk of him
              Pam's letter hasn't come.
I mean, it's come but can't be opened. It sits
in my email, obdurate, closed.

I read Tony's new selection. Many
I had read before. I still like best
the portrayal of his room, the pictures in it—
postcards, invites, a photo or two,
it resembles his mind, he says.

          A guy like 'Robbie'
from *Taggart* walks past. *Taggart*—
I hate that show. How unexpected
          to remember
'Robbie', tho the actor's jauntiness guaranteed it.
On the Flash's radio All Saints sing their big
          first hit
—what was it called? I always liked it. I bought it
          for Anna
gratifyingly long before it charted. Three or four
          midriffs
go by & a guy I know says hullo as he
sits down to his coffee & the paper.
Under one of the outside umbrellas
I see Apollinaire
sitting alone at an empty table—
he's wearing army gear—no helmet of course,
just a tiny canvas army beret, a little like
a mitre, appropriately, & his head
          —Picasso-style—
is tiny: the papal Apollinaire, in khakis,
an empty latte in front of him, those funny
WWI leggings around his splayed legs;
his little moustache, his perplexed features
tiny in the middle of his round round face,
a pear-shape: Picasso—cruel & kind. Time to go.

Central Market, May

Kate Deller Evans

Spanish music ignites shoppers
frigid in autumn's first chill

quickening through the
fresh peas and early mandarins

heralded with a wild precision
the circling couple a whirl

stamped feet of Flamenco
staccato clapped hands

aubergine-satined and lemon-frilled
spinning to riotous applause

Saturday morning crowd
revitalised, now able

to lug new loads, baskets of flowers
fragrant bunches of herbs, or pull

from favourite stall, the last
long loaf of bread before lunch

to head home with heady gypsy music
ringing warm through their skins.

Sharon

Amy T Matthews

'What does a Sharon look like?'

It was a game we used to play and Paul's way of welcoming me back.

He was standing at the bridal table, holding the bride's place card between his carefully manicured fingers. The air-conditioning ruffled his shoulder-length brown hair (carefully moussed and styled to look natural) and made him look like he was in a music video.

'Come on,' he prodded, flicking the place card back and forth impatiently, 'what does a Sharon look like?'

I sighed and took a break from setting out cutlery, the forks clenched in my fists. 'A Sharon? She's from the edges of Salisbury,' I paused and amended, '– the Heights or Salisbury North, not necessarily Salisbury proper – and she has a bad eighties perm, the kind that's all dry kinks that look like they'd snap if you touched them. She dyes her own hair so it's always too yellow and brassy, but she doesn't know what a toner is so she doesn't know how to fix it. She always seems to have a stripe of brown re-growth along her centre part, like a skunk stripe but reversed.'

Paul grinned at me, ignoring the bitterness in my tone, which crunched like gravel underfoot.

'Oh,' I added, feeling mean, 'and she's fat.'

It was my first day back and I was in a gloom; this was the nadir of my adult life. I'd quit waitressing the summer before, leaving with a flourish, bubbling with champagne and flinging my apron behind me, to fall where it may. Too busy counting chickens to protect the eggs. Ten months and a failed gallery showing later, flattened by bad reviews and worse sales, I was back. Worse, I no longer had a mental polaroid of my Great and Shining Future to sustain me. Instead I had the cold hard truth: I wasn't an artist, I was a waitress.

And not even a very good waitress, as Rick reminded me when I crawled to ask for my job back. He'd made over the restaurant again in my absence (which he did every three years or so, to stay 'current') and it was now called SubLime. The polished wood had been ripped out and replaced with brushed steel; the chandeliers were gone and in their place were angular curls of plastic; there were new white banquettes (white! Imagine the cleaning bill) and the back wall was a brooding black slab. Everything was black and white, stark and sixties.

'You'll have to do something with your hair,' he said, looking me up and down. 'We're going for the Mod look, you know? And lose a few kilos.'

Too demoralised to muster any moral outrage I went and got a gamine cut and lived on coffee and cigarettes until I was fashionably starved-looking. Still wanting to punish me for swanning out mid-shift in the middle of the summer rush, Rick only took me back for functions. And the wedding of Sharon and Wayne was my first.

They weren't our kind of people. That much was obvious from their table set up. Pale pink roses and gypsophola. None of us could help wrinkling our noses at the sight of it.

'Baby's breath? I didn't even know they still made it,' Paul said, looking at the stalks pearled with miniature fluffs of white.

'It's not *made* you idiot, it's a plant,' Elle laughed.

'Well, ick. It's like having sour sobs at your wedding.'

'Or salvation jane,' I chipped in.

'Or thistles,' we all said at once.

'Hey Elle,' Paul called across the room to where Elle was setting out starched white napkins, 'what does a Sharon look like?'

'A Sharon?' Elle pursed her newly filled lips, which glistened like fresh-caught fish, 'She's from Kilburn. Dropped out of school to be a hairdresser but still hasn't discovered what a toner is.'

Paul caught my eye and winked.

'Oh,' Elle added, 'and she's fat.'

Our games of Guess the Guest were never right. If we said Maureen was a maiden aunt with a blue rinse and a polyester dress she was bound to be a lean, power-hungry ad exec pumped full of Botox. If we said Gary was a mechanic from Tea Tree Gully he was bound to be the sports announcer on Channel 7, caked with orange make-up and strangled by a bad tie.

So of course we were astonished when Sharon came in.

The guests poured in half an hour early, to take advantage of the free drinks. They looked out of place amid the steel and plastic and I just knew we were in for a night of Jack and Coke and well-done steak. It doesn't happen often, because SubLime (or Bella Rosa as it used to be, or Utopia before that) is so expensive, but now and then we get a group that just doesn't fit. They don't understand the food ('What do you mean carpaccio is *raw*?') and they feel uncomfortable, which can make them belligerent.

This group was the definition of belligerent. Most of the men had guts like hard rubber, bulging over their belts. The ones who didn't were rail thin, with shoulder blades angling through their shirts like flightless wings. The women were colour coded according to their age – the older ones in dusty lavenders and sage greens, suits bought at Miller's or Harris Scarfe; the middle-aged ones bright as parrots in beads and sequins, hair blown into frosted puffs, necklines plunging to reveal cleavages ravaged by sun damage; the younger ones in black, long and short, cigarette packets clenched in taloned hands. Their eyes slid over us, thin and expensive-looking with our hundred-dollar haircuts, and something muddy bubbled in them.

I have never worked a wedding like it. There was no smiling or laughing. They made straight for their tables and started drinking. It was as though an invisible line had been chalked down the centre of the room – one side was Wayne's and one was Sharon's and they didn't mix. They were there to drink: sparkling white, cheap but fizzing with bubbles, for the older ladies; Bundy and Diet Coke for the young. The men were on beer and Jack and Coke. The wine bottles, lined up like soldiers, stayed corked and silent.

They'd all had a couple by the time the bridal party arrived and Paul stayed behind the bar, pre-mixing rows of spirits and Coke.

SubLime's enormous plate glass windows (tinted so we could see out but no one could see in) faced onto Hindmarsh Square; so we had a good view of the limo pulling up and the bridal party pouring out. A white stretch limo. Paul caught my eye again and winked.

The groomsmen got out first and didn't bother to help the bridesmaids. They were dressed in rented tuxes that were a little too short at the ankle, revealing burgundy socks. The bridesmaids struggled from the low car, wearing a slightly lighter burgundy and mushing bouquets of pink roses and baby's breath against the door jambs. Their hair was piled onto their heads in curls that looked plastic with hairspray; sprigs of baby's breath poked from between the junction of the curls. Everyone in the restaurant had paused to watch and I heard the only laugh of the day as one of the bridesmaids reached into the well of her cleavage and yanked her strapless bra up.

And then came Sharon.

She was big. A round ball of a bride; her flesh straining at an expanse of white duchesse satin, which caught the light like a mirror on a hot day, glaring unpleasantly. Her hair, the exact shade of polished brass, was hanging in a dry frizz around her egg-shaped face, topped with a tiara of roses rolled from duchesse satin and a short veil that fell to her shoulders, which rose from the strapless bustier like a rugby player's.

No one helped her out of the car or even looked at her.

Behind her came her husband, a lean guy with a short bristle of reddish hair and a can of West End in his right fist. His rented tux looked too big for him, the sleeves hanging down almost to his knuckles. He didn't look at Sharon and she didn't look at him.

The MC, an older guy named Ray with a walrus moustache and a tattoo of a bluebird on the back of his neck, announced the bridal party (which was weird, since we could already see them through the window). There was subdued applause as they tromped their way to the bridal table. As soon as they sat the DJ started up, loud enough to make the plastic light fittings jitter and dance.

They drank vats of Bundy, Jacks, beer and cheap fizz and ate charred meat and overdone fish (they sent the salmon back so many times, complaining that it was raw, that the chef, red-faced and cursing, plunged the lot of it into the deep fryer. 'Why don't you tell them to go to Charlie's?' he snarled at us).

It was only because I was working the bridal table that I began to see why they weren't at Charlie's; why they were spending buckets of money I doubted they could afford at someplace so hip and glossy. It was because of Sharon.

She ate her salmon rare, closing her eyes in silent ecstasy with every bite. She dipped her bread in the premium-grade olive oil instead of demanding butter. She drank only the Adelaide Hills sauvignon blanc, which I knew was one of the best on the list; crisp and green, tasting of shadows under spreading trees and grass bent double with early morning dew.

I saw her watching Elle. Elle who was as tall and thin as a sapling, with a long neck, pouting lips (not natural, but so well done it was hard to tell), and hair streaked in shades of ash blonde so tastefully it spoke of the three hundred dollars a month it cost to maintain.

As she watched Elle I could see another Sharon trapped inside this one, pressed against the hard glass of her eyes. This Sharon was wild-eyed and screaming like a banshee: '*That* is who I should be!'

The brassy frizz of hair, duchesse satin and baby's breath was who she was; the salmon and young green wine, the expensive chic of the restaurant and the style of its staff were who she could have been. And the Sharon inside was wailing.

After Sharon and Wayne had cut the cake, a three-tiered marzipaned affair made by Sharon's mum, it was time for the speeches. They were short.

The best man first: 'Here's to my mate Wayne and his new wife. May your fridge always be full of beer.'

A smattering of applause from Wayne's side.

Sharon's father: 'Well …' He was almost speechless. He fussed with his tie, which was hidden beneath a low and wobbling jowl. He looked out at the crowd and flushed a dull red. 'We all know why we're here.'

There was silence for a beat. People looked down at their glasses; no one smiled.

Sharon's father looked at Wayne, who didn't look him in the eye. 'At least he's done the right thing by her …'

'Omigod,' Paul breathed into my ear, 'she's *pregnant*.'

It was impossible to tell under the yards of duchesse satin and fat.

'People don't get married just because they're pregnant,' I breathed back.

'*These* people do.'

'So he's all right in my book,' Sharon's father finished, clearing his throat awkwardly. He proposed a toast and everyone drank. Everyone except Sharon, who kept her gaze on the wine glass in front of her, still half full of pale wine, shining gold in the captured light.

When she threw the bouquet no one ran to catch it. It thudded to the ground and lay on the dance floor, a ball of tightly curled roses and gypsophila fluff. It was still there when they left and I picked it up. The roses were bruised.

'What a nightmare,' Paul sighed after the last of them had left. He began filling a garbage bag with the table decorations; he held it out for me to toss the bouquet into but I couldn't.

'Do you know I didn't hear her say a word,' I said. 'Not one word.'

'Who can blame her?' Elle screwed up her nose. 'Did you see what she married?'

'Oh *come on*,' Paul snorted, 'did you get a look at her? She's lucky to get that.'

As I put empty glasses up on the bar I caught my reflection in the mirror. I was so thin the skin beneath my cheekbones was hollowed out; for a moment I fancied I saw a flicker in my eyes of a little me banging on the glass of my retinas, wailing.

What does a Sharon look like?

A Sharon looks like me.

Taking the Cake

Steve Evans

Terry drummed his fingers on the steering wheel. There was no parking to be found anywhere along King William Road, and he was already five minutes late. A middle-aged blonde in a blue silk scarf and designer sunglasses had just slid her convertible into the only space he had seen, giving him a cheery wave of condolence.

Never mind, today was a day for pleasure, a day for success. He recited his mantra: Mimi, Mimi, Mimi. And then it appeared; a florist's delivery van pulled out from the kerb right in front of him and Terry swung his Alfa into the vacated spot. Now he could make up the lost time. He locked his car and walked briskly towards the bistro on the corner. A quick call to the office on his mobile as he went.

'Tricia, it's Terry. I'll be at lunch with a client until … two. No messages, okay? Unless it's about the Atchison deal, of course. Okay? Bye!' What they don't know won't hurt them, he thought. Besides, he was to be a junior partner any day now. It was in the bag.

He checked his watch. Fifteen minutes to fix the surprise for Mimi, then say an hour for lunch with her, pick up Atchison at two thirty and show him the new apartments project, take him back to the office, a bit of smooth talking and Mister A would be signing on the line before the day was out. Perfect end to the week. Life was good!

Terry stepped into The Blue Hat, Mimi's favourite bistro. It was already beginning to bustle with the lunch trade, the suits and frocks. Terry spotted the owner at a customer's table and tugged her sleeve. She looked up, distracted.

'Hi!' he beamed. 'Terry Chalmers, for one o'clock. It's the corner table.' The one by the window, where he had proposed to Mimi.

'Ah, one o'clock? Let's see. Chalmers, yes, you're at the window.'

'Fantastic. Back soon.'

One more stop before Mimi arrived. Everything was falling into place.

Mimi. How was he to have known when he first saw her standing outside his office that she was the boss's daughter? Terry had been married once before, for two years, and had vowed never to do it again. But that notion was gone in an instant when he met Mimi; he knew immediately that she was *the* one.

It was funny how they had also known the minute they saw it that the cake in the window was *the* cake. They had been returning to their cars after a late-night coffee and paused for a kiss. As they were about to resume their walk, they had seen it in the window next to them – four tiers of iced ivory perfection gleaming in a soft light. Their cake. Terry wasn't exactly sure what it was that made this cake the only one Mimi would settle for, but there was no doubting her passion for it. And now Mimi had no idea that he had put a deposit on it. She would be so impressed. Today he would pay the balance and bring her back after lunch to show off.

The shop seemed empty. Terry coughed and rang the little bell on the counter. A woman entered from the rear kitchen, wiping her hands on an apron.

'Sorry,' she smiled. 'Short-staffed today. I'm covering back and front. What can I do for you?'

'I've come to pay the balance on the wedding cake for Chalmers. It's the big one in ivory; cascade of roses.' Terry put his receipt on the counter.

The assistant read it slowly, and gave him a look of sympathy that made him suddenly uneasy. 'Ah, Mister Chalmers. I'm sorry, Mister Chalmers, but it was damaged. An accident.'

Terry willed himself to remain calm. He had promised Mimi there would be something special today and there damned well would be.

'Well, okay … I suppose you'd better just fix it then.' He tried to convey the strength of his will in a gaze that was friendly but firm. 'It can be fixed?' He nodded, urging her to agree.

'I'm sorry but it can't be done.'

'I'm sure with some icing and all that, it won't be noticed. It's just a cake.'

'No. It was quite a smash.'

This wasn't what he wanted to hear. 'Look, she … my fiancée had her heart set on that cake. If it's a matter of money, I'll pay.'

'We had to destroy it.'

We had to destroy it? She made it sound like a horse. Jesus, thought Terry. Right, stay calm. 'Well … okay then, make us another one.'

'I'm sorry, Sir, but our cakes are unique. We never duplicate them; it's a policy.'

'But it's been destroyed, suffered some catastrophic event. It's a non-cake.' He felt as if he was trapped in a Monty Python sketch. 'If you make another one that will be unique, won't it? It will be the only one.'

The woman leant her hands on the counter and shook her head.

Terry leant forward too and spoke softly and slowly. 'Get it back. It's mine.'

'I have another very nice cake that you'll really like. I'm sure your fiancée will adore it. Here.' The woman left the counter and moved over to a display stand in the window where a ziggurat of jagged icing sheets towered over them. 'See, it's also a four tier and it has these lovely wreaths of …'

'No.'

'Look, in view of the trouble, I could knock 10 per cent off the price. But you'll need to settle on it now.'

'No.'

'I'll even deliver it.'

'I want you to deliver the cake I paid for.'

'Well, to be fair, you must admit you only paid a deposit, and each order is subject to availability.' She turned over Terry's receipt and pointed to a mass of incredibly small print. 'It's all in our terms and conditions. And we can't deliver the one you ordered now, it's gone.'

'Gone! I thought you said it was destroyed.'

'Same thing. It was damaged and it will be destroyed. We can't have broken and second-rate goods going out of this shop. We're professionals, after all.'

'So, it's still here then.'

'I didn't say that.'

'You mean you won't say.'

'I'm not selling a damaged cake. We have our reputation to consider.'

The door opened as another customer entered. 'Please think over my offer while I see to this gentleman. Now, if you'll excuse me just a minute ...'

She left him standing by the giant fractured iceberg he had just rejected. It was imposing but it was a completely different style of cake. He had promised Mimi a surprise, but not this one. Terry checked his watch. His appointment with Mimi was in five minutes and she was not a woman to be late. She would be at The Blue Hat any moment and watching for his arrival. He had no time for all this stuffing around.

The woman walked into the rear of the shop and emerged carrying a large pink concoction on a tray. It looked like something for a kids' party, but really expensive. Still, those two things went together in this neighbourhood. The other customer held the front door of the shop open for her.

'I'll just be a second, Mister Chalmers. When I've helped get this into the Folkestones' car, we'll sort out your order, okay?'

Terry stared at the cake in the window. He gave it a short angry punch of frustration, and it broke like an ice floe on one of those tedious documentaries about the Antarctic. His hand went right through the flimsy outer layer and stuck firm. He tugged but his watch had become snagged on something; his hand wouldn't come out. He tried turning his wrist sharply to each side, hoping that whatever had caught on his watch band might disengage and let him withdraw his hand unnoticed. It just hurt his wrist.

He looked up to see that a man on the footpath outside had been looking at him through the window. How long had he been there? Terry smiled politely and wrenched his hand free. The base of the cake was simply icing plastered over a platform of cardboard, wire and some sort of filler. Inedible. No wonder it had snared him. There was a raw pink line on his wrist.

He remembered sliding his fingers around the curve of his mother's mixing bowls when he was a child. The sweet delight of sticky fingers. There had been something naughty about it, even if he had been permitted the indulgence. Terry shook the thought from his mind and brushed broken icing from his sleeve. Well, definitely not this cake, he decided. As he turned back to the counter, he saw something unexpected. Through the doorway that led to the work area in the rear of the shop, he could see a bench. Sitting on it was a cake that looked exactly like the one he had ordered.

He glanced out into the street and saw that his recent spectator was gone. The shop assistant was some distance away, her bottom poking out of the rear door of the Folkestone BMW as she secured their birthday cake. Terry darted into the rear of the shop.

It *was* his cake! It had to be. They only made one-offs, she had said so herself. He circled it quickly, checking for signs of damage. There was nothing wrong with it at all. The bitch! She'd obviously bumped him for someone who'd offered more money. Did she think he wouldn't guess? Okay, okay. What now? Think quickly, Terry. He could see the side-alley through a screen-door. Right, no one fucks with Terry Chalmers! He pulled out the envelope with the rest of the cake money and dropped it on the counter. His cake, no damage, money paid – a done deal.

It was heavier than he had expected. He had to lean it against his chest as he pushed the door open with his foot and stepped out to the alley. Walking, if you could call it that, meant looking around it and down to one side to get a sense of where he was going. He had to make speed, though, and get some distance between himself and the cake shop before she came searching. With any luck, being short-staffed might mean she would have to stop to lock up first.

Terry emerged onto the main footpath, nearly bowling over an Unley matron in the process. She exploded with a loud, '*Really!*' and huffed away.

His car. If he could get the cake safely into his Alfa, he might still get to The Blue Hat in reasonable time. The cake was becoming more difficult to carry. It grew heavier and his arms strained. He chanced a moment to lean against a post and re-balance his load. The top tier was out of kilter but he managed to brace it under his chin. One of the pillars was sinking into the icing. Terry pushed himself away from the post, carefully glancing back toward the cake shop for any sign of pursuit but there was none, so far.

The cake shed a little rose of icing as he walked on. It shattered on the path and fell into the gutter. No way to stop for it. Can't bend down. Keep focussed on the car. Get to the car.

The cake began to bow increasingly as Terry lugged it along the footpath. He needed to rest somewhere. He retreated slowly, backwards, into the doorway of a clothing shop, trying to move out of the line of sight of anyone who might be following. It occurred to him that he would hardly be able to sprint away. He needed a new strategy but he couldn't think of anything. In the meantime, he rested his back on the window.

Move, move. He shrugged his arms further around the base to get a better hold, curved his shoulders inward to brace the upper tiers, and stepped back onto the path.

All things considered there hadn't been too much wear and tear on the journey. There was icing all down the front of his jacket, yes. Some had also come off the decorative ring on the top and smeared his chin. No matter. Smooth out the rough bits with a knife. Dry-clean the jacket. His legs, though, were leaden and his hands slippery with sweat or something else coming off the chocolatey surface of the cake, but he was going to make it. He could see his red Alfa just a block ahead. Get the cake into the car, tidy up a bit and duck across the road to The Blue Hat. Nearly there.

The second highest tier began to slide. Terry instinctively ducked his head so he could hold his cheek against one side. He felt exhausted. He told himself to count his steps. Break a job into small achievable chunks and tick off one part at a time. That way just about anything could be done.

Finally, he was there. The cake hadn't suffered any further, though he was walking like Quasimodo on dope – a very tired Quasimodo. He pushed up against the passenger door of his car and sighed. He even allowed himself the pleasure of closing his eyes a moment, still clinging to the cake. It was while he was in that state that it occurred to him – he didn't know how he would open the car door. His shoulders lost strength. To have made it this far …

Terry forced himself to stiffen. He turned slowly and began to lift the cake onto the roof of the coupé. His knees trembled with the weight and it was clear that the structure would not hold. He lowered it again carefully, tipping it back slightly against his chest for security. Then he tried moving forward just far enough to place the edge of the base on the bonnet of the car instead. He balanced it with his left hand while reaching for the door handle with his right. Please don't be locked.

It wasn't. The door began to open, and the cake began to teeter. Terry froze. If there was a passer-by, he could ask for help. This woman?

'Excuse me …'

But she stared straight ahead. He thought he even heard her sniff at him as she passed. He was about to abuse her when his mobile phone rang. Mimi? She was ringing to find out where he was. No, a bit soon for that. Jesus, the apartment deal! Four million dollars riding on the afternoon and Atchison chooses that moment to call.

There was no other way. Terry hauled back on the door savagely and simultaneously lunged to save the cake. The whole thing seemed to undulate for a moment but then its movement subsided.

The phone kept ringing but at least the door was now open. Terry hooked one foot under the floor-mounted lever that would allow him to slide the seat back and make room for the cake. Jesus, he thought, you'd want a photo of this; standing with one foot in King William Road, balancing a four-tier wedding cake. Not likely to happen again. The phone stopped ringing. Now he had his foot under the lever but couldn't work out how to actually push the seat back at the same time. He would have to put the cake in the seat as it was.

The phone rang again. Terry knelt down and slid the cake through the doorway. The top tier caught on the roof of the car, the second tier caught on the seat belt, the third tier caught on the edge of the seat, and the bottom section capsized in his hands. The whole ragged heap slumped into the passenger seat, a three thousand dollar wreck of white chocolate, cream and sponge filling.

Terry pulled his mobile phone from his jacket just as it stopped ringing again. He tore his jacket off and threw it into the car, slammed the door shut, and punched up his work number.

'Trish, what? That was you, wasn't it?' He wiped his sleeve across his cheek.

'You don't need to be so gruff with me, Terry.'

'Just tell me, will you?'

'No, it wasn't me. I think you'll find it was Mister Parker. He's joining you and Mimi for lunch and couldn't find you.'

Terry sagged. 'It's all right, Tricia. I see him coming now.' He hit the off button, folded his phone away, and gave the approaching pair a little wave. Mimi was bubbly, her arm tucked into her father's.

'Terry, Terry! You'll never guess. It's so wonderful!'

'Mister Parker.' Terry nodded at his boss and future father-in-law, and tried to position himself to block any view into his car.

'Hello, Terry.'

Mimi pecked a kiss on Terry's cheek. 'What's that on your chin?'

'Nothing.' Terry whisked his hand across the offending bit of cream. Mimi didn't seem to notice; she had something else on her mind.

'Daddy is such a sweetie. You know that wedding cake we really liked? Well, Daddy has done something amazing. When I told him about it yesterday, he went straight to the shop and bought it. It's his present to us.'

Terry's legs evaporated. He propped himself on the Alfa.

'Well, I knew it meant so much to my girl,' said Mimi's father, and gave her a hug. 'Someone else had put a deposit on it but I made what I would call an irresistible offer. Paid an extra thousand.'

'Oh. Good.'

'Terry? Are you feeling okay?' Mimi squeezed his hand.

'We can share lunch,' Mister Parker continued. 'Mimi's taking my car back home afterwards, so we can pick up Atchison in your little runabout together. Okay, Terry?'

Terry managed a kind of smile. 'Actually, I'm having a bit of car trouble at the moment. Would you mind if we caught a taxi?'

'No problem. In the meantime, let's all go "visit the cake"!' Mister Parker extended his arm to his daughter and they both laughed.

25 Fashoda St, Adelaide

Graham Rowlands

Squatting under the English elm
in the African street of
19th-century Empires
French against English
English against French
I'm cleaning up leaves

not the falling & flying
autumns skittering across green
but dry old grey leaves
piled between climbing wire
& corrugated-iron fencing.
I'm pulling out handfuls
along with toy metal cars
minus the PR of their paint
faded plastic science fiction
a heap of plastic pegs
that will scrub up – those
not unhinged or snapped off

& tinged with blue-green
this heavy chunk of glass
thick, rough & shapeless. It
shouldn't have worked its way up
through old grapevine soil
under the English elm.
It shouldn't be here.
The elm shouldn't be here
& neither should I.

WEST TERRACE ANGEL

Annette Willis

Fight, fight!

(Janet Charman, *Lessons from the Waitakeres*)

Cath Kenneally

she was a beautiful
woman, your mother
Moira said

did they tell
her that?
probably, knowing Moira

i hope mum
took it
to heart

she was nicer
to her students
than to us

Saint Aloysius College
where she went
to school herself

would never
badmouth the nuns
though

they bundled her off quick smart
when the time came

she didn't get
much older

fluttering against the windows
like a trapped moth
with dad gone

only still for
games of 'May I'
with her sisters

with no one to fight
she went to jelly

we didn't predict that
should have been cheekier
kept her dander up

The Aunt's Garden's Story

Nicholas Jose

The front verandah was wrapped in wooden shutters that made a cool antechamber to the cave of rooms where Miss G had lived for eighty years. The shutters protected her from the busy street. The first of their kind in the colony, they were a distant precursor of the now ubiquitous plantation shutters and had earned the house a place on the heritage list. Like a curtain across a stage, the slats made Miss G into an actor when she stood out front, expostulating to passers-by in knitted cardigan and cap, and stretchy leggings under a long full skirt, regardless of the season. Being hard of hearing, she spoke too loud, making people stop to listen. Then she would go inside, disappearing from public curiosity. She was private, lived always alone, worked professionally until retiring age, never married.

The woman would go through her old stone cottage to the garden at the back that was her haven, where the trees that she had mostly planted by her own hands had grown their fill: walnut, fig, peach, olive. Lawn curved around under the trees where flowering shrubs and creepers and clusters of pots – iris and agapanthus, salvia and geranium – filled the beds. All those years she had tended the garden, digging, watering, clipping, sharing that world with cats and birds, possums, butterflies and sometimes a snake. It had the look of a damp climate garden, yet also, with aloe and cactus, acknowledged the arid terrain. She weeded, bent double like a penknife, even into her eighties, to yank at roots as stringy and fibrous as herself. With her elbows on her knees, Miss G could rest her palms on the ground, leaving no gap between upper body and firmly planted legs. Concealed like a temple courtyard, the garden was a place of mystery, while cars and buses rushed past outside. When she was in the mood, she would socialise on the street, mornings with the postman, afternoons with office workers striding back and forth. She boasted of the history she had seen, insisting any listeners pay heed. She gave her opinions forthrightly, excoriating change.

A new townhouse was built next door, its high concrete wall casting an overbearing slab of shade over her garden. Miss G had lost the fight against it, as we discovered when we moved in. Without knowing it, I had come into her world as a spy, a watcher from above who could borrow the well-tended green view of a neighbour's garden. The woman hated being observed. Sometimes, remembering the invasion, she would look up and scowl. The perfectly established garden was her life's work. I had taken possession of it with my gaze.

I found out she had been secretary to the general manager of a large company. She was no pushover. Then one afternoon in September a storm came with a ferocious wind and blew down the cypress pine at the front of her house, crushing the heritage verandah. Miss G lived frugally, according to her needs and habits. When the council told her that the verandah must be repaired in keeping with its original quality and design, largely at the woman's own cost, she would not play along. Instead the old arabesque iron roof was tied down with rope and the place made to look derelict. 'It should just be demolished,' one morning walker declared. In that battering of pride, how Miss G's body and spirit must have suffered. She was dead a year later.

Through the next summer her nephew and niece kept watch over the place from a distance. They lived interstate and the problem of their aunt's house was now theirs. People came in to water the garden and keep the grass green. Then the property went on the market. The condition of sale was that any buyer must restore the fallen verandah and heritage shutters. The facade must stay intact. But heritage did not extend to the larger envelope of the house. No value was given to the garden, or to the memory of the person who had created and cared for it, inseparable from the house in her understanding. And no regard to the benefit a neighbour gets for free from a vision of delight.

The new owners were quick to adapt the site to their own conception. The second summer after Miss G's demise and the first summer after the sale of the property, the garden was removed. The hot, hard work was determinedly done in a matter of weeks. Loyal to Miss G's memory, the postman intruded at one point to photograph the old peach tree as it lay scattered across the ground in chainsaw chunks. A hundred growth rings ran under my fingers as I felt the cross-sectioned slabs of that rough warm wood. Then everything was taken away and the site was cleared.

Let in for the first time in nearly a century, the harsh summer sun lit up the wall behind for all to see.

The earth is level now. The magpies are having a good time finding worms in the rich red soil. As the space is prepared for the next stage of construction, no trace of Miss G's rare old garden remains. Its peppertree, its lemon, have gone. No one documented the site in any particular way before she died. Although I have the best view of it, I never took the time to record its details through the changing seasons. There never was that time. Perhaps I idly imagined that my love of it would bring about a stay of execution? I suppose I thought that the value I found in what Miss G had done in her long lifetime would be recognised sufficiently to save the garden. Now, as the digging starts for the new foundations, it feels as if her grave is being turned. Her spirit floats homelessly on the air. If she could see, she would stand in the street, in front of those old shutters, in front of the passing cars, clench her fists and howl for all to hear.

So Long, Dianne

Kristel Thornell

It was a beautiful face – maybe more exotic than classical – that used to make boys skittish, with something absent-minded or distant about it. The bones had become more assertive, as if her face were a sculpture that was finally complete, everything superfluous at last whittled away. It was consummate, Kat decided, in a way that young faces weren't.

Otherwise, Margot was as she remembered. She had the same bearing she'd always had. At uni, a 'mature-aged' student among eighteen-year-olds, Margot had prematurely assumed the attitude of being *d'un certain age*. It had suited her then and still did now that it wasn't an affectation anymore. Kat said the strange numbers in her head: we're fifty and forty.

A couple of weeks in Adelaide – a kinder, less self-involved city than Sydney – would be good for Kat's 'convalescence', Margot had insisted over the phone, as though divorce were an illness you could reasonably expect to overcome with a bit of human decency.

They drove off from the nowhere of the airport in a borrowed car with a dog in the back of it.

'I don't believe in driving anymore. I cycle to school, everywhere. The carbon footprint, etcetera. Are you *okay*, my dear?'

It was summer. The air felt so much drier than Sydney's – there was always this comparing, the inability to see except by way of the old, as if peering at the new through the window of your own familiar house, which you don't seem able to leave. The light was completely unrepentant. The old Honda, in which they were barely sweating, moved against a vast backdrop, uncluttered, so wide-open.

'How are you really? Before you tell me: let me say how over the moon I am you've come. And another thing. I always knew he wasn't for you, Kat. I blame myself.'

Kat silent, Margot continued: 'I don't know if I came back because of the divorce. My divorce.' Kat remembered the end, quite smooth, apparently, of her friend's shortish marriage to the bank official. 'Maybe I was just over Sydney. The anger people get around with, you know? That toxic loneliness.'

When they were studying French at Sydney Uni, during those years that were allegedly the best of their lives, Margot almost never mentioned her native Adelaide. Kat intuited an escape from an airless family of rich conservatives. Her friend downplayed the habit of privilege, but it was clear in the confident shapes of her words, an offhandedly stylish use of scarves, food snobbery and her uncomfortable laughter at jokes Kat belatedly realised had been crass, working-class.

The odd times Margot talked of the city where she was born, it was of good-mannered, monotonous mildness that sounded to Kat, a survivor of Sydney's prickly west, potently foreign. She hadn't travelled, hardly at all, even in Australia. She imagined Adelaide as a place existing not so much at a different point on the map as at an earlier moment in history, virtually mythological, where a golden age that Sydney had long since forgotten – if it had ever known it – continued to flourish.

Margot's neighbourhood wasn't far from the centre of town. They cruised the main drag and a few of the more picturesque streets, to give Kat a feel. There were hairdressing salons, lots of them. It was pretty, gentrified. Houses related to one another across space. Kat stuck her head out the window to breathe in the placid affluence. Edna the dog did too, starting to whine. Many houses sat behind brush fences: picture-perfect heritage bungalows, all compact, appealing geometries and radiant sandstone. In a genteel daydream, Kat lounged on one of those verandahs with some kitsch iced drink, guiltlessly idle and possibly intact.

Margot's house wasn't as old as these, but was still from a time when architecture was elegant. It was too big for one person and not something a teacher's salary would pay for. Family money. Or the divorce settlement.

Apologetically, Margot said, 'The inside's a bit run-down.'

In the front yard, there was a tree with orange bark that made it seem lit by a violent sunset.

'The drought's been bad,' Margot commented as they moved along the side of the house. 'All my friends are rampant greenies.'

Margot showed off the compost heap. Kat studied the mound of tealeaves, eggshells, banana and mango skins and slices of mouldy bread, interested in the disruption of smoothness by the occasional jutting angle. The fermented smell was rich, barely rank.

'If you had a different idea of ripeness,' she observed, 'that'd be a feast.'

Kat the teetotaller. It was a running joke at uni; these jokes exist to lubricate the machinery of student life. She was seen as lame for it. Which was ironic, because she'd grown up in proximity to drinking, so for her not drinking was the subversive, interesting act. But by the time she was sitting opposite Margot in a pub on Hutt Street, she'd learnt to drink enough to make a decent display of it.

They started with a local Shiraz – soft, warm. There were berry notes (Kat snickering at herself, the wine connoisseur!) and something far less innocent; a distance behind these. A certain plush darkness she was more and more inclined to topple into.

After ordering cognac, Margot confided, 'I've been on antidepressants for a bit. It can take them a while to find the right … *medicine*' – she said it voluptuously – 'and to get the dosage right. Then a while for it to kick in, but when it does, well, it takes the edge off nicely.'

Margot made this speech buoyant. She managed to be consistently upbeat. Kat had the old impression that Margot met disappointment with incredible grace. If this involved a huge effort of will on her friend's part, she made it invisible. Margot was a mysteriously comforting companion, her manner some sort of flippant melancholy or grave playfulness.

'Should you be on the grog?' Kat found nothing better to say.

Margot shrugged. 'You'll like it here. It's a cliché, but Adelaide really is so much less uptight. Doesn't take itself half so seriously.'

'Also looks good through a rear-view mirror,' the waitress offered self-deprecatingly, bringing the cognac.

'Don't get me wrong,' Margot said, sipping from the small glass with an ease Kat couldn't replicate. 'I love Sydney. Sydney's lovely. A stunner. If the cities were people, Sydney would be the knock-your-socks-off knockout, no question, but Adelaide's the … you know, quieter, not-so-flashy beauty in the corner. Who grows on you. The one you end up stuck on. I've turned into a regionalist.'

'I see your point,' Kat began, discovering that the way to drink cognac was to moisten her lips with it, then wait for the burning to die away, moving forward in tiny increments. 'I don't think I've ever got under the skin of Sydney. It's never been mine.' She tried to gaze at her friend attentively, gently. 'Could be a class thing.'

Kat's thoughts hung in opaque veils through which she squinted at the next one. For a moment, she saw this scene they were doing – her and Margot playing old friends chatting, getting drunk – as it unfolded on a movie screen. Look, Kat observed to herself, there I am not long after my divorce in a bar from a quaint past. The projector was caught and the film was starting to burn through. The hole was Kat's mouth, flaming with cognac.

'This harder stuff is not for me,' she said.

'It's good you never had children.'

Kat agreed. 'I was probably infertile.'

'Oh, darling.' Margot reached out and touched her arm.

Kat asked herself if straight women were so free with endearments for one another because their involvement with men left them starved for them.

Margot warned: 'It's not the best idea to go through the parklands at night.'

Then why were they doing it? Were night-time parklands the

kind city's shadow? Kat felt jolly and subtly disembodied. She savoured the weirdness.

'There's a more direct way,' Margot complained, gesturing to an area barren of trees that had to be a sporting oval. 'But there're the bloody racecourse fences. Like the circles of hell! You have to get down on your hands and knees to go under them. It's a tad humiliating.'

Instead, they took an asphalted path leading through lines of very tall ghost gums. The only light came, somehow, from the gums, a muted glow as you approached them. The trees were like benevolent inhabitants of some Other Side, offering their supernatural luminescence to those still shambling through the living world.

Margot said matter-of-factly, 'You don't have to talk about it.'

Margot was custodian of Edna, a medium-sized Spaniel, and Charlie, a smaller, shorthaired mutt of thirteen, who'd been preparing to die for months. Edna was excitable and portly, an eater from hands, while Charlie mainly lingered in the corridor, wheezing faintly, and had to be helped onto the bed, where he was finally allowed to spend his nights, having been punished for this vice all his life.

Charlie had gotten excited – or disoriented, which was the form his excitement now took – when Kat arrived in the doorway with her suitcase. He'd seemed to recognise her.

'Oh!' Margot had exclaimed. 'He thinks you're Dianne.'

It seemed that Charlie, never the sharpest knife in the drawer, even in his better days, had taken Kat for his and Edna's previous owner.

'You do look like her, Kat. Tall. The fair hair.'

Kat wasn't offended by this case of mistaken identity; it confirmed her own uncertainty as to who indeed she might be in this place. She appreciated the attention she got from Charlie.

After going 'a bit off the rails', Dianne had come to stay with Margot for a time. This was clearly a pattern for Margot, welcoming the lost into her home. When Dianne moved on, overseas, she left the dogs. Margot grumbled about them, but cooked top-grade meat, letting it cool before diligently mixing it with kibble, and tended Charlie's last days with devotion. She was incredulous, however, that Dianne could have taken her friendship so casually, shot through, not stayed in touch. Margot worried about Dianne and Kat wondered if the antidepressants dated from Dianne's departure. For two years, Margot's garden shed had held Dianne's discarded possessions: a box-spring mattress, a crummy bicycle, books (suspense novels, Anaïs Nin, volumes on ancient Egypt), a mannequin wearing a kimono.

'She loved those dogs.' Margot mused. 'How could she abandon them?'

Perhaps it was relegating Dianne's things to the shed that left the guestroom so bare, an echo chamber. Kat thought of that Leonard Cohen song: 'I choose the rooms that I live in with care, the windows are small and the walls almost bare, there's only one bed and there's only one prayer; I listen all night for your step on the stair.' And the chorus, which went, 'But I know from your eyes and I know from your smile that tonight will be fine for a while.' The jaunty melody didn't fit with the song's breaking heart. From the guestroom's single bed, Kat heard footsteps as loudly as if she were in the corridor; these seemed more than could be accounted for by the house's inhabitants.

There wasn't much sleep to be had during the close nights. Kat pondered the word *close* and this heavy sensation it described, thinking of poor Bruce and how it'd been necessary to become remote from him. Lying awake, she was afraid to disturb Margot, who the next day had to face other people's teenagers, most indifferent to the subjunctive and fickle French pronunciation. With Margot at school, Kat napped with the heat as her alibi, just getting up for the loo and to check on Charlie.

'You're okay, mate,' she crooned.

Another oppressive night. Margot and Kat had eaten their sautéed wild mushrooms and perfectly poached eggs and were already cleaning their plates with sourdough bread when the lights went out. Blackouts occurred on days like that, the city's electrical supply unable to take the collective retreat into air-conditioned denial. Kat felt her way out to the compost heap in the gloom. Incongruously, the neighbours were filling their garden with lanterns.

'We picked a great night for the party!' The stocky man, whose name she'd forgotten, had caught her peeking over the fence. 'I'm the birthday boy. You girls can pop over, if you'd like.'

'We were about to turn in.' Kat was embarrassed. 'Many happy returns.'

The party made the farce of sleeping even more of a farce. Lying on her back with her palm against the cool wall, Kat listened to the crowd growing next door, gleeful or sarcastic greetings, the festivities taking shape in the dark. Eventually the cake (wickedly decadent or funny) was carried out and the song started amid hilarity. A speech of elusive tone followed and finally something unexpected: a string quartet tuning up.

Kat got up, knocking over a candle she'd left on the floor, and went to find Margot, who couldn't be sleeping through this.

She found her meditatively polishing off leftovers by candle-light. Edna's quality of attention showed she'd been helping. Margot hummed with her mouth full, as if knowing the tune.

'Bach,' she commented, after a moment.

'The lights aren't back on?'

'I forgot to try,' Margot said. 'On Sunday, we should cycle to Henley Beach. You can take Dianne's bike. It works. Want some?'

'I'm full,' Kat replied, but found the raspberry jam that tasted of lemons and whose colour in daylight was divine, psychedelic. 'Fridge light is on,' she announced, though Margot didn't respond. Kat spread the jam on the remaining crust.

'I had the best fig of my life a few years back from the public market,' said Margot dreamily. 'The perfect fig. I haven't had one to match it since. It makes me think of fishermen fixated on the big fish that keeps getting away.' Margot fondled Edna's ears and added, 'You don't sleep much.'

'Not really.'

Margot had heard her these past nights, rolling back and forth on the decrepit bedsprings. The music and the jam had calmed Kat, but now she felt awkward and exhaustion seemed to return to the front of her skull, a pained murmuring. She recognised the beginning of what she angrily thought of as hysteria. Its logical endpoint was weeping, but she wouldn't cry in front of her friend.

Margot wasn't quite looking at her. 'Tu veux pas venir dormir avec moi et les chiens?' It was the first time someone had spoken French to Kat in around twenty years. The voice in the other language was oddly intimate. 'It'll be cooler in with us. We've got the fan.'

Kat fumbled along the corridor and toward Margot's big bed. The sheet was thrown back and Charlie lifted his tired head ecstatically to receive her, breathing into her face.

Charlie at the end of the bed, Edna lay between them, under Margot's arm, like a child. Kat didn't draw away from the dog's animal clamminess. The fan sounded like an old-fashioned aircraft battling to ascend.

Kat hadn't hoped for sleep, only to be soothed, but she was soon flirting with a dream in which Adelaide was a name for middle age: an intensifying awareness of death, but also a large gentleness. She saw a Dalíesque plain on which indignities were transformed like melting watches by the enormous radiance.

Margot encouraged her to venture into the hills or at least take the tram to Glenelg, but Kat had energy only – maybe like Charlie – for modest discoveries. The map she liked best in her travel guide was of the simple grid of the inner city. It gave her a sensation similar to that of staring into a radio battery from which the back has been removed. There were the clean, orderly pathways the current would take.

In her second week, she started going to the nearby park with Edna in the evenings after Margot had settled into planning the next day's lessons with a cold glass of white. At the park, Edna was reborn as herself amplified. If the same couldn't be said of Kat, she felt different, delicately, pleasantly alien.

The day turned tolerant, the tail end of sunset was the time for walking. The light lowering, the heat finally showed some compassion, becoming inward and sensual. The foothills were a blue you could perhaps call tender. The colour made Kat think of the skin under insomniac eyes, of certain bruises. She didn't return to the path through the ghost gums. Occasionally, human forms bobbed above the ground in the dusk, athletes doing push-ups. A vision both military and balletic. Once, she and Edna came across a man playing bagpipes. And inevitably, there were lovers in pairs, lying under trees in confusing arrangements of limbs, joined by biological or more arcane instincts. Kat wondered how dry hot air affected the thoughts of desert peoples: did it placate mental activity to a smooth baseline or make it shoot up into areas above the graph? She guessed thought would acclimatise to dry heat as to anything else.

When night proper arrived, some dogs had lights on their collars that signalled invisible frolicking. Kat had found a way to cross the park straight through the centre, but heading home preferred to confront the racetrack's oval fences. When she went down on all fours, Edna was pleased by this admission of a secret quadruped nature.

Charlie greeted their return, gazing at Kat with tremulous joy. She took this to mean, 'Oh, Dianne! It's been so long, I thought you were never coming back.'

Picking a Fight with Colonel Light

Michael Winkler

Query: Why has there never been a decent boxer from Adelaide?

I have theories, I suppose, but no evidence worth the name, says the careful woman with the overweight wheeze, eyes small and brilliant, mouth downturned against the next disappointment. We could talk about the non-convict past, about the patterns of migration, about pathways for those below the lower rung by dint of socioeconomic accident or indigeneity, and there might even be something somewhere in all that. We could, perhaps. But not really my area.

Well *we* don't know, say the girls in preposterous party frocks, high-heel wobbling and hailing the taxi, champagne giggling, the same Brighton beachfront Cup Eve party as last year, and actually the same as the year before that, the calendar's clunk an unwelcome corsage on this night of planned weightlessness. We don't know boxers. We don't like boxers!

I know – in fact I'm certain – it's got to do with the light. (This one: smudged jeans and broken RM boots.) Have you seen our city in the afternoon? I've been in planes at that time, looking down; I've been in Alberton and Thebarton and Goodwood looking up: the colour evades me yet. There is orange in that afternoon light, and blue, too, but I puzzle with it daily and resolution gets no closer. If you can help me out, pin that colour with a name, you couldn't imagine …

Who are ya, poof? Where you from? Kenso boys rule, you faggot. Whip any eastern state fags. (The greedy motor roiling like a cauldron. Tyres fat and lovingly blacked, mags shined like icons, the car all muscle. Preening. The strobed gaudiness of Jetty Road popping from its glistening duco. In an hour or two the petrol boys will pass the champagne girls as they tumble from their party; looks will be exchanged, but nothing more – nothing except sound: roiling exhaust carolling to hollow party's-over screams as they move rapidly, inevitably, apart.)

Is it true is it true he asks, bush around his jaws, a broken canvas hat, plastic dark shades, who is it says there are no good boxers here? Sorry – not ever? Well this does come as a surprise. Um; now give me a moment now. Applying a gap-toothed rake to his memory. The pause long enough for the smell to stick; sweet medicated sweat, bad beds, rubbish. Creaking to the pie van on North Terrace while he thinks on it, but the day is too early and the pie van is not there. Over the road is a convenience store, and down the side is that good pizza place, but both are waved away. I'll get back to you, he says.

Well if there aren't there bloody ought to be. (Beer-fat, skin stretched across wide cheeks, nicotined hair like hotel room curtains either side of his bare head.) When you get blackfellas you get boxers. Ones in the city here, can't pick any more if they're desert blacks or the Africans from Somalia. Um Sudan. One, anyway. A widening chink of probability that he will say it'd get them off the welfare or give 'em something to do or their skulls are sure thick enough for it. But he says no such thing. Shrugs away instead and is thinking, it seems, of sadder things already.

The heft and surge in the stands at Hindmarsh. Because it's a mug's game, yeah? Because there's no future in it? We're too smart for that bullshit over here? The sun-addled denizens of the hill end at The Oval. Haven't really thought about it. Can't say it worries me! Good shot, deserved more than one.

No kickboxers either. No MMA. No muay thai. No fists in skulls, no pulped up faces, no leer-lipped boozehounds looming from their seats calling vanquished boys weak dogs after they've lost on points.

There was a trip to Bridgewater for memory's sake. Drove past the house, twice, back and forward, checking it was actually the one, the trees so much bigger now, and something different about the verandah. Perching in the green air, elevated from the complexity of the lowlands, taking a night on impulse in a fussed-up Piccadilly B and B. Asleep before either intended, then waking in the black blue, the bare window a frame of bright 3 a.m. sky, and fucking quietly, quiet, because who would know what to say at breakfast if the owner was listening in. No one could make love like that in a fighters' town.

It doesn't fit the culture (from one young enough to be certain). Oddly proper, jade lip-ring and all. This is an arts city. A community of intellectual risk. Lots of combat, all of it creative.

In winter the rain weeps from the hills, and the city is enveloped from east to west in water, and people hovering on the fringe of great desert know that at these times they share something bigger, and they feel an unspoken thankfulness. Gratitude, reverence.

We've had Paul Kelly, Neil Kerley, Don Dunstan. The Chappell boys. People want to come here. Coetzee is up there somewhere now. Nobel winner. Tim Flannery came over, the arts festival (we started that craze). Three AFL premierships since '97. This bullshit about trying to run us down. Do you understand why we get sick of it?

Why hasn't there ever been a decent boxer from Adelaide?

The question is wrong. It implies a non-existent importance. There are factors that impinge on all manner of things, pugilism the least among them. View this from Whyalla. View it looking back from a boat jogging the horizon in the gulf. View it from the eyes of your children in ten years' time. Like the question, the angle is wrong. Better to screech of the homonymic aptness of Skycity and Scarcity, the brooding darkness of the governor's residence scowling over the commerce of town, the sounds of skateboarding ghosts outside the courts at night. Everything is contingent.

May as well say – may, as well as anything else, say: there has never been a decent boxer from Adelaide because the Torrens keeps its secrets, its ancient Kaurna secrets, its dead child secrets, its Christmas night illicit love secrets, its tormented suicide-struck introvert secrets, its secrets smooth between perfect twin green banks. It keeps its secrets close and chooses flow. It might suggest that you do too.

The Dumbest Thing Christ Ever Said

Rob de Kok

After Chris's farewell barbeque Phil made me go with him to the Land of Promise. He said it would be good for me and it was good because I met the man who had found God. I might even have met God, I don't know. The Land of Promise is on Port Road, and on a Friday night there are women there who dance and shed their clothes gently for money. And they sell tickets for this and men are chosen to be the one on the chair in the middle of the back room while the dancers play, stark naked, on their bodies. It seems that the men have no active part in this at all – they just momentarily become somewhere for the women to dwell, rendered powerless by the ritual. Most of the men have their hands behind their backs while on the chair and they seem sort of happily embarrassed.

So I ran into this guy there and right off he says it was his seventeenth visit to this place. It makes sense now – seems that it takes about three months for someone to get evangelical about something cos straight after that he said he was there to worship; that the back room of the Land of Promise was his church, a place where God dwelled and was made visible and took human form for a moment and gave us back something for all our sufferings. And I said where's this God then, being smart, and he said she's the next one to dance, after this one – there, the one with the genuine blonde hair and no make-up, and I made the mistake of laughing a little. He showed me his bible.

It was his own personal bible, handwritten over four months, a collection of a dozen or so 48-page A4 exercise books; the top one the most scrappy, the bottom one the most recent, the newsagent's smell still on it. He had stuck them all together by gluing and stapling cover to cover so the whole thing had the feel of something more deep and important. There was a picture of Pamela Anderson at her most gross on the cover. He said it was his bible. The books of his bible were called The Fifties, The Sixties, The Seventies, The Eighties, The Nineties and Now. There were four gospels called Matthew, Mark, Luke and John. John was this guy's name. I found out later that Luke was his son's name. There was no book dealing with the future – there would be no raising of the dead in his bible. Now I recall it there seemed to be no Old Testament either. It just started at The Fifties, his Genesis, and it started with 'In the beginning was the world.'

I didn't read much after that because the music for her dance began – it was Dire Straits, that slippery saxophone opening phrase – and for her entire act John stood and watched in silent rapture, although the punter the blonde was dancing for didn't get as much as an erection out of it.

Then we drank while he talked. He said he didn't mind not being the one on the chair tonight – it made no difference in his eyes, as long as he attended while she danced. It was rare for me not to interrupt but he was so scarily certain of it all that I knew this was real for him and for me perhaps a potential monologue or character study some day.

Turns out his house in Walkerville had been made over by the *Backyard Blitz* team two years ago. He had organised it, taking his wife and kid on a small fake holiday – he went too – while the scrappy cubby house was bulldozed and the desolate yard of tricycle tracks and discarded toys was transformed into some place with a deck and a water feature. He'd made it happen. He'd nominated for it to happen – for her – and he couldn't wait for the homecoming moment, couldn't wait to see the expression on her face. She was knocked over – there's still footage somewhere of her face fiercely contorted by surprise and joy, her words small clouds in the cold night.

Three months later their relationship was over. It took him another two months to find his wife and another six to ask her what the fuck had happened. She didn't say, but from her sister he heard that the *Backyard Blitz* thing had really spooked her.

You see, she knew nothing. In all the phone calls and the planning and the chat about the holiday and excuses for that trip and the casual conversations while on the Gold Coast or Bribie Island or wherever – in amongst all that happiness – she knew nothing. He'd handled it brilliantly (he was quite proud of it at the time) and she knew nothing and it hit her while she was hanging up the washing weeks later what this meant: it meant it was possible. She could exist outside of his zone, and he outside of hers, and if that could be the case for *Backyard Blitz* it could be the case for anything.

And from that moment Trust left their side. Now, Hal Hartley says that respect, trust and acceptance are all a relationship needs but forgot to add that they work together like legs on a milking stool – no matter how uneven the ground is, three legs will stand steadily. It's pure geometry, really: any three points can exist in one plane. But take just one leg away, the leg labelled Trust in this case, and you'll fall on your arse. In John's bible, in the Book of the Fifties, it actually says 'Respect, Acceptance and Trust, but the greatest of these is Trust'. I asked what about Love and he said that the word 'love' doesn't appear in his book.

So John came home one day and his wife was gone and Luke was gone and most of the furniture was gone as well. A week later he set fire to the new deck in the backyard. You might remember that it was in the paper cos the fire spread to a neighbour's brush fence and anyway you're not supposed to burn that green treated wood and the sharp smell of arsenic hung over that part of Walkerville for weeks.

John spent a year on the street and in sheds in Port Adelaide trying to get his view of the world back. But all he got was angry. And when he was ready he went to the Land of Promise for revenge. He was going to buy a ticket a week until his name came up for the chair. He was going to buy a ticket to make a woman, any woman – it didn't matter at that stage – do her whole dance, perhaps wait until she was actually standing on his thighs, perhaps off balance, and then break the rules.

He made up his mind to grab her and go as far as he could, given the watching crowd and the security staff out front. That was what he had planned to do. When I think of it now I figure that he just wanted something simple. He wanted to get the shit kicked out of him in the hope that, afterwards, there would be no more shit left in him. It's not that uncommon.

But, that night, it never happened. What did happen was that he found God. That first night he drew the true blonde, just by luck as it turns out, although, to read it now in his bible, that's not just a random thing any more to him – nothing is now – and she did her dance and took off the little she had on and by the time she was completely naked John had undergone his own Saul to Paul thing and knew that there was no turning back to Damascus. Revenge went out of his head and in its place were all the components for a God-system he now explains as there from birth but not unveiled until the blonde was there in front of him without a stitch on.

He said he'd never seen a woman naked before – not his wife, not even anyone he got close to in his stumbling youthful years. I didn't understand how this could be but he went on. He said in that naked moment he realised – and this is the core realisation for him – he realised that he had never actually seen a woman before in his life.

I'd had a few drinks by this point so I went to a toilet so old it still had those sweet cubes in the urinal and, to be honest, on the way back, I was half-hoping that he'd be gone but he was still there and he hadn't latched onto anyone else. Phil seemed to have deserted me so I knew I needed to see this story, this theory, out.

According to John none of us actually see women – this is one of the things that clicked for him that first night in the back room. We don't see them, we just see an image they carry around all their lives. And all of his life till that moment on the chair he had thought that the image was it, was them, but it wasn't. He had a sort of epiphany of pure flesh – a credo, a revelation, if you will.

And, in the same way that those boring-again Christians

trawling for stray souls in Rundle Mall will tell you that the information you needed to truly understand and truly believe was in the back of your mind all along, that something's been nagging at your thoughts and they can name it for you right now and the name is 'Jesus' – that's his name and he's been there all along as the quiet, waiting unspoken grasp you needed on life – in that sort of way John, the guy in the bar at the Land of Promise, knew at that moment that his Unspoken had got him to this transcendent point.

And his Unspoken, now spoken to me, ran like this: she's not that tall; that's not the colour of her face, that's not the colour of her hair, that's not the shape of her hair, that's not the shape of her eyebrows, that's not the size of her eyes. That's not what her breasts really look like, that's not her true silhouette, her fingernails are not real, her lips are not that shade of red. In that space he met a woman for the first time, saw her as she truly was. And he realised that, for that minute or so, the woman in front of him had nothing left to hide, nothing left to reveal. And she was left untouched, as a deity should be.

So, after that first time, everything was in place for his conversion – all lined up in his head, and it just took a little trigger. Three days later he was getting groceries at the IGA and was backing his car out of its space when he saw in the rear-view mirror a sticker on the window of a red Ford Laser behind him. The sticker was purple with stars on it and it said 'The Goddess Is Dancing' and John put his car back into its space and sat there on the boot and waited for the owner of the red car to arrive.

She turned out to be a woman with henna hair and a clear face and she actually owned a shop on Goodwood Road which sold the stickers – she was picking up some bulk supplies for it – so he followed her there and it smelt like Nag Champa, wheat and lanolin soap and he asked for a sticker and she asked why and he told her that he actually knew where the Goddess was Dancing and she made the mistake of laughing a little. He showed her his bible.

By the time he'd left, four hours later, they'd decided that 'do unto others as you would have them do unto you' was the dumbest thing Christ ever said; that that bit of John 3.16 which goes 'God sent his only begotten son' is a curiously specific turn of phrase harbouring an obvious ambiguity, and that the purple sticker he was buying was, in fact, technically wrong. Face it, the henna woman said, how can someone who won't use the words 'hostess' and 'actress' subscribe to a similarly diminutive term such as 'Goddess'? But John got a sticker anyway, and it took until he got back to his place at Alberton before he realised that he'd forgotten to pay for it.

It isn't long before a simple, straight-up belief gets lonely, gets in need of a bigger circle of influence. And when that happens it looks for ways to convince others, a crazy concept if you ask me. From epiphany comes the ascribing, the trap of the written word, and from more visits John constructed pages which he thought this simple moment needed wrapped around it to keep it warm and alive in his mind and make it transfer easily to others.

He gave the moment context and defined his recollection of it. He created a 'Why' for the 'What.' Between visits he remembered and wrote, but there in the back room of that pub, or on the chair, with nothing separating them, it was as simple as he had once wished for. Each Friday he knew the truth – the word really was made flesh. He knew that the woman before him had the power to speak and not to speak, to offer and not offer, to choose and to strike down, to take and not take, give and not give. She had the power to create life itself and the power to destroy it as well, and he realised that his happiness was inextricably tied to hers and for the length of that song – always the same song, 'Your Latest Trick' – he could sit as her domain, sit serenely as part of one of her worlds and feel momentarily that she was part of his. And he knew that this was the way it should be: the hidden, the untouchable, the nameless, the one who can never be understood, the Mystery.

I made up my mind to go to the Land of Promise again the following week and see how John was and how his work had grown and to see him in ecstasy just one more time. It could be his lucky night

– he could be chosen again – and I wanted to take his photo. But I didn't ever go back and anyway, cameras aren't allowed in his church.

I never found out the name of God. Phil said she was called Victoria but others said her name was Michelle or Celeste or Ali or Sarah, Lisa, Shanti, Jasmin or Cal; depends on who you ask, but when I'm in the Port area I'll be keeping a look out for a car with a purple sticker on it, a shorter than usual purple sticker which says 'The God Is Dancing'. When I see it I'll be able to say: see that car – that's John, he's the man who found God in the Land of Promise.

On Reading an Electrical Meter at the House of the Rising Son

John Tranter (writing as Mark Pallas)

(*Transit* No 1, September 1968)

In the twenty-fifth year of my age
I find myself a Ford at Bomaderry
the tank dry, starved between
one collision and the next garage.
Adelaide flames and howls under the horizon
lighting up a petty testament of waste.
Apart from the moment of accidental vision
the dull grey trees stand about
inclined to olive, drab, cold, gathering in trembling clumps
under the lowering field of cloud.
You are not alone in this Southern desert;
love, like a wounded elephant, terrible and pathetic
storms the deadly streets to hunt us down.

Note: I have always regarded 'Ern Malley', the hoax poet concocted by the young James McAuley and Harold Stewart in 1943, as an early master, along with Slessor and Webb, and the appearance of his complete *oeuvre* in the *Penguin Book of Modern Australian Poetry* was long overdue. The ambiguous beauty of his poems may now enchant schoolchildren as it once did me. This piece, published pseudonymously in the *annus mirabilis* 1968, argues with Malley's 'Petit Testament', copying the first line exactly, parodying the first quatrain rhyme for rhyme and almost word for word, then branching off into a loose criticism of Australian literary life in the forties in a way that reminds me of A.D. Hope's ambiguous jeremiad *Australia*, with a bit of Jacques Prevert (the Rod McKuen of French surrealism) thrown in at the end. Malley's opening line, by the way, is taken from Pound, who took it from François Villon. Here's Pound's poem 'E.P. Ode pour l'Election de son Sepulchre', Part I, last stanza:

Unaffected by 'the march of events'
He passed from men's memory in *l'an trentuniesme*,
De son eage; the case presents
No adjunct to the Muses' diadem.

Oliphant Avenue

Shannon Burns

It is not hard to get lost in familiar surroundings. Especially if you are, like me, somewhat withdrawn, inhabiting perpetually a space inside yourself, with its own architectural dowdiness, if you are reserved, in other words, for a place that is continually calling out your name, whose flowing invitations find their echo in the pulse of your veins and the heaviness of your throat.

So it was, at that time no less than the moment of 'inscribing' it on the imaginary sheet in front of me, this illuminated imitation of the bodily presence of a page, upon which my words slide back and forth and mutely interpose themselves with dried tears and unrefined hopelessness. I am here, the words say. But what am I?

Even a ghost needs a home to haunt. And if the spectre has no home, if it wanders around directionless, unsure of its own reality and unable to root itself in the certainty of place – whether that consignment be the nightmare from which it refuses to depart or the soil upon which all of its hopes have depended – what then? It becomes the ghost of a ghost, the pale, stricken cousin of the vitality that is ghostliness, the meagre remembrance of what it might have been to be that way, to have lived in the world in the first place.

So it is with me. I have been a ghost for a long time. I mean to say a *real* ghost. I am flesh and bone after all. I will not be conjuring metaphors here. Rather, I will attempt to be as precise with words as possible.

How did it happen? How did I come to be a ghost in this world? Well, it's very simple really. At the moment of my death I decided to live. That's all. Without any real reason, which is to say meaninglessly, I accepted my death and lived on. Whether I have lived *despite* my death or *for* my death I have never been able to decide. There is, perhaps, an extent to which I have lived on in memory of having wished to live, as a sort of testament to the fact of my once hopeful existence, of what I had been and what I might have been, just as a scanty rag or a tuft of leaves might bear witness to every departed hope torn loose in the whirlwind.

To live on despite being dead. That is all it is to be a ghost. It has something to do with the withdrawal I was talking about moments ago.

I have always been withdrawn. Opening up to the world, I have been taken from it. When my father was informed of my birth he drank heavily and merrily. He shouted to the rooftops of his pride and I have never been anything more than the echo of those shouts. Everything that has been given has at the same time shown itself as fleeting, as being given only for a time, which is to say *not to me* but to a moment within which I have been present. Those moments have taken everything from me. I am like a head peering out at things from a time portal or another dimension. My body will never experience any of it. It never has. It is lost to me.

Again: I have always been withdrawn. If I am to be honest with you now, as I have intended to be all along, I must confess that the main reason for this withdrawal, for my tendency to live inside myself and my tendency to get lost in familiar surroundings, is that I have poor eyes. I cannot see properly. I have trouble focussing. If I am to be even more honest, to be painfully upfront with you on this score, I have to admit that everything significant about my life has been subject to this deficiency. All that I've lived through and thought, every encounter, all of the ecstasy and dejection, is a simple reminiscence of this failing.

I see things differently. Which is to say nothing more than this: *I am a child of poor vision.* My mother gave my fate away one day as we were walking across a field to my grandparents' house. She squinted hard against the bright horizon and said, 'Is that your uncle?'

I never answered her question. At that moment all I could think to say in response was, 'What's wrong with your *eyes?*'

Why? Because I knew what was in store for me. When your vision is faulty, everything looks otherworldly, glazed, *wrong*. Faced with the spectacle of my mother squinting ludicrously across a field, and despite being no more than nine or ten years old, I felt certain that I was destined to live a distorted life. And I nearly wept with that presentiment.

Place names have meant very little to me. I've never given them my attention. I am always forgetting my address, phone number and age. There is something about my situation that makes all of these things airy to me. They are not part of my withdrawal. They have nothing to offer a distorted gaze.

But Oliphant Avenue was memorable. Living by that strange, damaged road, a swerving plateau of public housing refuge, I found my surroundings oddly familiar. It was easy enough to get around from there. Oliphant Avenue. was my compass. This was probably the case, to be honest, because it sounds like *Elephant*. I have no trouble remembering animals. If all of the streets, suburbs, cities and countries were named after animals, I would always have them on my mind and I would never stray far from my course.

This is perhaps because animals are perfectly withdrawn from us. They inhabit the same uncertain world as I do – a world of mirrors, teeth, warmth and misplaced trust. They have been tossed out on the street, destitute, dissociated. Everything has been taken from them. They can be destroyed as easily as the inclination to murder them arises. No one will stand up for them. If they are ghosts, then they are ghosts of a world most people doubt ever existed. They are the inhabitants of Atlantis, the sunken world of earthly promise. If our streets were named after them, I say, I would remember. But what use would that be?

I'd been living on Oliphant Avenue, with my sister and my little nephew, for around six months and everything was going exceedingly well. I had been a ghost for nearly a year and I was in the peak of physical fitness, having become a member of the local gym. I was working long hours at the recycling depot and spending a great deal of time at the beach, at nightclubs and in bars. My skin was wonderfully smooth and brown. I was miserable, but forcefully so. I was lingering, strangely, ridiculously alive, and I had decided to embrace the farce of my existence completely.

I was nineteen and I had a smallish bedroom, of which the bedding was the main feature. I had a queen-size alongside my old single bed. Together, they took up about seventy percent of the floor space, combining to create a gigantic bed-room, which was met, I'm sure, with a mixture of delight and horror by the young women who were confronted with it.

There were lots of them. I *was* miserable, but also very fit, tautly sculpted, and exceedingly persuasive. However, my failings with regard to orientation and remembering place names extended to remembering the names and faces of people, and this was the cause of some discomfort.

Sleeping with girls and women was never enough to make me remember them. Not just because I was often quite intoxicated, and not just because my vision was very poor. Rather, it was because they were, as it seemed to me, completely contentless. They were creatures upon whom I performed spectacularly, as a trapeze artist might stretch and twirl and contort the ropes of his profession, but they were also unmistakably frail. Some of them would look away in a sort of passive horror while I was upon them, and others would cling to my back for dear life, as if there were something I could do to save them from the heartbreak of their predicament. Night after night my bed-room bore witness to calamity heaped upon calamity. It was a disaster zone and I was an Angel gazing out at the ruins. Its storm blew me along with it and I was powerless to do anything but watch and embrace the destruction.

But I'd always forget the disaster the next morning. I would forget *everything* about it, including the faces and names of the girls and women – the virgins and mothers – from whom the catastrophes were extracted. Nothing of them remained.

Again, I remind you that I am being literal and attempting to explain the situation with as much precision as I can muster. I forgot *everything*. I was blank repetition, a Don Juan without a scribe, a ghost in hell on Oliphant Avenue.

It was in the midst of those ruins that something strange occurred. It was a rest night, which is to say I hadn't arranged for anyone to come around and be set upon. On such evenings I often read a book. At the time I'd been reading a biography of Napoleon Bonaparte and, mysteriously and quite by chance (as it seems to me now), a small collection of the works of John Ruskin. However, on this particular night neither option seemed appealing.

So I grabbed my phone and made some calls. I had a pile of numbers from girls and women who hadn't yet made it to the bed-room. Their names were, of course, handily attached to their numbers. I liked to ring them when I was bored just to see what their reactions would be. It was my practice to put very little effort into my relations with women. I knew that, on most occasions, those who had chosen to give me their phone number in place of coming to the bed-room on the night we met were bound to be more trouble than they were worth. Such was my understanding at the time.

The phone calls were going well. (As with everyone, women enjoy the idea that they haven't been forgotten. It matters very little who does the remembering.) But I held out no hope at all as I made the fifth call. It was a friend of Michelle's, the buxom blonde who was dating my best friend. Michelle had seen me go home with other girls and women on numerous occasions in the two weeks since we'd met, and it seemed to me that she was bound to inform her friend of those encounters and ruin any chance I had of luring her into the bed-room.

I made the call, however, and we spoke for three hours. Nothing like it had ever happened to me before. She asked me where I lived. 'Oliphant Avenue,' I said. 'Oh, like the scientist?' she replied. 'I'm not sure,' I said. 'I thought he was the governor.' She gave a delightful giggle and we arranged to meet up on the weekend.

It's been five years since we met and I have never informed my wife that she is living with a ghost. I don't think she's noticed – and if she has, she doesn't seem to mind. We're very happy. We've been married for a year. We live in a small apartment and have four plants: a Kangaroo Paw, a Blue Lagoon, a Peach Lily and a Bonsai. All of them are extremely healthy and well cared for.

The other night we went to an award ceremony at the university. My wife was receiving a prize for the best mark in a law course. She has recently finished her bachelor degree and been admitted into the profession. Our sex life is wonderful, yet I'm incredibly miserable. Such is the way with ghosts.

During the ceremony, as she was strolling up to receive her award, I was reminded of the fact that I adore my wife in a manner that is constantly surprising to me.

The guest speaker at the ceremony was a female chief magistrate, in the matronly tradition, who'd graduated from the university more than twenty years ago. After spending a good deal of time reminding us of the difficulties women have faced over the years in the pursuance of legal careers, she asked us to consider our heroes. I was tired and decided not to obey, but after a few moments she began to talk about her own 'hero', as she called him.

During the late 1970s, she said, I had the honour of working as an assistant to the then governor of South Australia, Sir Mark Oliphant. Mark was born and grew up near Adelaide at the beginning of the twentieth century, and was very keen on science as a young man. He had a middle-class upbringing, with a civil servant for a father and an artist for a mother. He studied right here at the University of Adelaide, she said, and was taken in by the enthusiasm of a lecturer in physics. After hearing a speech on radioactivity and the atomic nucleus by the eminent New Zealand physicist, Ernest Rutherford, she said, Mark's career was entirely mapped out before him. He wanted nothing more than to spend his life uncovering the mysteries of the atom. Upon winning a scholarship to go and study in England under the supervision of Rutherford in the mid 1920s, Mark began his work on the artificial disintegration of the atomic nucleus. Like many of his fellow researchers at the time, Sir Mark was forced to design and build much of the necessary apparatus for his experiments, the most notable of which was probably a large particle accelerator called a cyclotron.

The machine was responsible for taking a subatomic particle and speeding it up, thereby generating particle energies between a few million and several tens of millions of electron volts. It achieved this, she said, via the use of electromagnetic fields. It would then fire the particle into an atom and break it apart.

In 1932 Mark's fellow researchers were responsible for bringing the count of particle-types in the atom from two to four. He was surely overjoyed when James Chadwick identified the neutron and Patrick Blackett discovered electrons with a positive charge, thereby proving the existence of anti-matter. It was an exhilarating period for researchers in nuclear physics, and Mark must have felt a mixture of delight and relief upon making his own revolutionary discoveries. His contribution came in the guise of two new forms of hydrogen, deuterium and tritium.

This discovery led directly, said the chief magistrate, to the development of nuclear weapons and the creation of the hydrogen bomb. During the Second World War, she said, Mark worked tirelessly to persuade United States officials to implement a programme for the development of the atomic bomb. The programme was approved and he would ultimately work directly on the development of the bomb itself. When two of those bombs were finally dropped on Hiroshima and Nagasaki, she said, Mark fell into a state of shattered disbelief. He said at the time that he had never imagined the bomb would actually be used on human beings.

Sir Mark was a kind man, she said. He was a humanitarian and a significant figure in Australian public life. He was also a vegetarian and abhorred the mistreatment of animals. From a young age he had been deaf in one ear and suffered from severely poor vision. He was diagnosed with astigmatism very early on, a disease which causes aberrations outside of the optical axis.

When Sir Mark began his research on nuclear physics, excited and enthralled by the prospects of the science – an enthrallment he had caught from Rutherford in 1919 – a complete understanding of the atom was thought to be the stepping stone toward a better understanding of the universe and, as it seemed to follow, of the creatures that inhabit it. The fact that the destruction of the atom, the violent tearing apart of matter, was necessary to understand its mysteries did not seem to provide any portentous forewarning to the participants in its ruin.

It was said that Mark became a vegetarian after seeing first-hand the gruesome slaughter of pigs when he was a child, an image that haunted him throughout his teenage years and made it impossible, on some nights, to sleep. In his later years he was known to associate the terrible squealing of confused and horrified livestock with the sounds emanating from the cyclotron as it did its work. The knowledge that he had put the machine together with his own hands, using the bare essentials available to his under-funded laboratory, haunted him endlessly. In his later life, said the chief magistrate, Sir Mark was a passionate critic of nuclear weapons.

And it is with all of this in mind, she said, that I want to tell you that no matter where you set out from, no matter what your intentions, it is likely that, many years from now, you will look around and discover that you have strayed so terribly far from where you thought you were headed.

Those final words of the chief magistrate, which had the effect of muting and disorienting her audience, seemed to me, at the time, to be a wondrous way of explaining, quite precisely, the feeling of distortion and decay that has beset me throughout the years, both when I was alive and in the ghostly existence I've led beyond my death.

THIRST

Anne Bartlett

Cityscape

Matthew
in the lift
going up
and down
up and
down sees
a coloured
poster
pimping
great escapes
to other cities
other lifts
going up and
down up
and down
two thousand
smackers
round return
three nights
accommodation
one travel
bag for free

rubric cubes
narrow tubes
climbing cones
flattened angles
smoggy circles
basic blocks
bare squares
enclose liaisons
not lovers
persuasions
not passion
tightly screwed
covers
no fathers or
mothers
plain parenting
people
or wrinkled
old bones
labelled
discreetly
in homes

shallow-rooted glass
castles mirror
dry weather
(slight heaves
of earth's crust:
will babble in Babel
buckle and topple
to domino dust?)
daytime mouse
Matthew hurries
on homeward doors
in blank walls
revolve and revolve
and revolve as night
falls to neon.
    Matthew scurries
buys curry
yearns over some-
thing broken
and nameless
sates it with cable
sits at his table
drinking and gaming
chatting (for real)
dreams dark in his
small coffin bed

stone
church
points
heavenward
squat
square
feet
cobblestone pub
oh God our help
in ages past

only
the
birds
fly
or rest
on some high
grimy sill
windows only
open half an i
so Matthew
cannot take a
suicidal leap i
that great free
of human hist
down below
hopping
sparrows find t
sweet sultana
dropped from
plastic snack
bag one
extravagant fr

at the bottom of banks and business buildings plump grey rats race run
riot bite and fright and cannot see the sun
    under beneath below earth groans and weeps and waits

Thirst

She met him in the lift.

Hi, he said, ignoring the rules. Saw her. Smiled at her. Knew her. Even the puncture marks on the backs of her hands, the other veins tissued long ago. Saw everything.

Where can I get a drink of water round here?

Didn't he know anything? Water? What a joke! He was surely an overlord. But he might do, all the same. Why bother with rules? Rules could break as easily as glass.

She answered.

Well, the cooler broke last year and has never been fixed. but what's the point? it was damn awful anyway, that biocycle regurge stuff from the sewers. there's still coffee or coke but fruit derivatives are cost prohibitive. no milk for years not since the cows were engineered to death so it's drugs or nothing sweetie pie though I'll show you a favour or two if you tell me how you have the gall to ask for water. never had the fresh stuff myself though they say it's good. they're importing recycle suits now so you only drink your own sweat not other people's piss. I can't afford one of those, though they say the advantage is purely psychological.

You're thirsty.

Sure I'm thirsty always thirsty. you can never get enough to drink. like you get enough to keep you alive but not enough if you know what I mean. they say the ancients had a rite called bathing. immersed the whole body in water. I mean can you imagine the waste but oh the luxury of it. water flooding your body wetting all the skin at once. I suppose it was at least a couple of cents deep. sometimes I dream of swimming.

Where's the river in this city?

River. River. I've heard the word I think. oh river. ah yes water. that's it one of the old words for water isn't it? are you some kind of priest or something that knows the old words tell me then. no don't fuss what I really need is credit for another score how's your credit status? mine's dead.

You need water.

No it's OK thanks I really need credit. got any creds? just a couple? actually I'm going up to see my sister she'll pay to see me go. nearly at her level now. bloody long ride isn't it. they say if the city keeps growing we'll hit the surface soon and we'll all be fixed for good.

I'll give you water.

hey who are you mister? where you from? not polite to talk to strangers round here. got any credits? I'm running dry and feeling funny.

I am the river.

Yeah but will you give me a fix? nup thought not. you're not the type you get to tell after a while.

One more fix will be too many.

Yeah well what's it matter not much choice right now just one more time too far gone and gotta take things slow I'm good you know been on this stuff for ages know it well I'll tough it out and cut back soon

You're dehydrated. Come.

This my sister's level. thanks it's been nice talking for a change see you later mate have fun with your river god sure you haven't got just one small cred? OK see you I'm gone.

Counting Chant created by children at Towers Child Care Centre

This little girl
She said one
One person rules and the others are dumb
Tot up your credit and count your cents
Put your money in the bank without pretence.

This little boy
He said two
I've got tons more money than you
Tot up your credit and count your cents
Put your money in the bank without pretence.

This little girl
She said three
They taste like vomit but nutrition pills are free
Tot up your credit and count your cents
Put your money in the bank without pretence.

This little boy
He said four
Kill all the others so there won't be war
Tot up your credit and count your cents
Put your money in the bank without pretence.

This little girl
She said five
Too many people but the clever ones survive
Tot up your credit and count your cents
Put your money in the bank without pretence.

This little boy
He said seven

They told us lies about God and heaven
Tot up your credit and count your cents
Put your money in the bank without pretence.

This little girl
She said eight
The world is poisoned and it's far too late
Tot up your credit and count your cents
Put your money in the bank without pretence.

This little boy
He said nine
I'm purebred what's your genetic line?
Tot up your credit and count your cents
Put your money in the bank without pretence.

This little girl
She said ten
When the song is over we must sing it all again
Tot up your credit and count your cents
Put your money in the bank without pretence.

The listener

Stephen was one of the first impaired children they let live. Mutations were becoming more common and it was increasingly difficult to draw from a pure gene pool: Stephen's profound hearing loss was less of a problem than other disabilities. Besides, he had a capacity rating of 12.839, double most kids his age. A pity, the professionals said, that he couldn't be cured by surgery. All that sensory input lost.

At the Towers Child Care Centre he didn't care for the prescribed chants, though he valued the ditties of the children's underground. The children allowed for his deafness and were straightforward in their speech; the adults prevaricated, and mostly forgot he was deaf. When they remembered, they shouted, as though that would make a difference. He lip-read early and well, missed nothing in sight. Finely tuned to vibration, he often picked up movement behind him, preferred to go barefoot for the purpose of 'hearing' more. He was a natural observer and could, when it suited him, blend into the background. He was fitted with a synthesiser so that his voice was less distorted, but he didn't understand the meaning of tone. He only talked when necessary. A friend, another loner who had a stutter, taught him to read.

Although he was deaf, and the words of the chants bored him, he was fascinated by their rhythms. He could see it in the bodies of the chanting children, feel it in the beating of their expelled breath. He developed a passion for understanding this strange phenomenon. He had never been exposed to music of any kind, not did he have any concept of musical instruments, of what it might mean to play a harp, press violin strings, push the slide of a trombone, to have such resonance quivering through him. Few knew those old things any more. Those things were lost. Those who knew them were inclined to think of music as a kind of black magic. *Music* – the word was a curse now, the province of shamans and illegal practitioners. If you admitted to enjoying the rise and fall of sound, you were strange, unreliable. A well-lived life was disciplined to one soft steady hum, the tiny ebb and flow of smooth machinery. Sound beyond this range was gross, macabre, bizarre, suspicious. Those who were anxious or stressed bought one-note hummers to calm themselves, to drown unpleasant sounds like birds, and learned to speak in even monotones. Children were rigorously trained.

Stephen, cut off from even these bland sounds, learned to amuse himself in various ways. He liked to be alone, and when he was fifteen he secured insular work as a junior librarian. It wasn't long before he discovered the archives, vast underground warrens of shelves and drawers, and volunteered himself for cataloguing. No one else was interested – enlightenment was not in the past or in the future but in maintaining the even hum of the present. Nevertheless, records were kept 'just in case', though even this practice was debated. After a few months Stephen came across pages and pages of manuscript paper, parallel lines covered with dots and hooks and curling flourishes. His supervisor told him, quietly, that this was 'music', an archaic language, better left alone. Soon after, Stephen was moved to another area.

But Stephen, methodical, deliberate, spent his rostered eighth day off studying the shapes and patterns on the musical pages until they spoke to him. He loved the mathematics, slowly began to understand the interplay of bass and treble, tones and semitones, harmony and dissonance. He knew he lacked a sense that others had, and guessed it was connected to these flowing characters. Meanwhile, he watched stressed colleagues flipping out their hummers. One woman said she envied him his pristine ears.

Slowly Stephen translated the patterns, deciphered the meaning of rests, quavers and semiquavers, dotted crochets, trills, runs, arpeggios, took increasing delight in chromatics and the simple squat shape of a semibreve. With an ancient children's theory book he learned that sets of lines were called *staves*, and that a colon at the end meant *repeat*.

One day he dropped his pencil. Pencils were clumsy, so little used now that they were rare, but he loved their ancient slender lengths, collected them, and used them on his Eighth Days. This particular pencil was a short red stub, five cents long. He had been holding it in his right hand, his left as usual lying flat on the table surface and his bare feet planted squarely on the floor, so that he felt the pattern of the pencil vibrating on the table and into his skin. And he suddenly understood that the patterns indicated movement and rhythm in another dimension. It was, he thought, like moving from 2-D to 3-D, or suddenly discovering the meaning of time. Yes, partly it *was* time. But also something else.

He went back over all the music to beat out the patterns. He loved the quick ones, but they were difficult. He could never drum his fingers fast enough. It was fascinating, and addictive.

Two weeks before his seventeenth birthday he became ill and fevered. In his eagerness to understand the patterning he had neglected his health. In twenty-four hours his skin, inside and out, broke into tiny blisters. His legal guardians were not concerned, but when it seemed he might actually die, they called in healers. The healers shook their heads and gave the water rite. There wasn't any water, so they used cleaning spirit, but what would the kid know? He was pretty much out of it, not one to talk.

Stephen was barely conscious. But he remembered later that when they left someone else came in. Someone gentle, with cool, kind fingers who touched his forehead. Immediately the pain eased. His head was lifted. Something deliciously smooth and cold washed down his ulcerated throat.

His right hand was taken, turned palm up. There was a pause, an invisible silent beat. When Stephen thought of it later, he remembered it as a view over a precipice. A strong finger, deliberate and precise, beat a rhythmic pattern into his outstretched hand.

At first it was simply pressure on the skin, but then something new began happening, something inside his head, something building and growing in time to the drumming fingers. Suddenly, like fireworks bursting in the dark, his ears were opened so that he was filled with sound. He knew immediately that this was *music*.

It stopped.

The loss of it frightened him more than anything ever had. And then he heard it again, slight as a breath, one note, two, an octave a little louder, two octaves, major key, minor key, dancing chromatic, repeating that very same journey he had taken through the fluttering pages in those first days in the library. An aching minor chord brought tears to his eyes, but before he could weep it resolved into another, deep and satisfying.

Silence.

He waited, no longer afraid. The strong hand grasped his own, palm fused to palm. Without warning the full orchestra was in his head. The music crashed and boomed, swooped and soared, scattered and clustered and fell in silver sparkles, then gathered itself into a great tidal wave of sound that carried him out to sea.

Two nurses found him lying still as death.

'Looks flushed,' said one.

A beam on his forehead.

'Reads normal.'

'Blisters down. What do you reckon? Sleep or space rattle?'

'Hard to tell. Used up his sickies. Have to bump him if he takes much longer.'

'Oh, one more day. Might be a genius.'

'Sweetsop!' Laughter.

'Not me. Just had it with disposals. It's my birthday.'

'This once, then. Just one day.'

They left.

Stephen opened his eyes. He had heard every word they had said.

Thirty credits for our one year anniversary

Thirty credits
My week's wage, my love,
Is yours to spend.

An antique bracelet?

> quaint paint on metal
> inscript Holden
> ancient travelform
> it suits your skin
> my dear, highlights the glint
> of green gas in your hair

this redgum box?

      Extinct and one cent square

      warm wood

a friendly dog?

      turdless plastiform

      walk-insistent

      bonus trim and tone

      off switch

      beats a baby

how about a holiday?

      three full days

      perfect bubble air

      imported from Andromeda

or just this once

      this grand extravagance

      (a long relationship

      deserves the best)

      payment for the safety pod

and mating skin to skin?

Love Apples

Have I ever told you about my sister-in-law? Such a sad case. Harmless, but a sad case. I tried for years to help her but she wouldn't have it. Too fertile for one thing. Too many kids, popping them out like plastipeas. Three of them, all the same, no doubt about parentage. Quite boring really. You'd think she'd spice up her life in that department, even if she neglected other things. But they had the right genetic combo, my brother and her, were paid well. Wouldn't think they had good genes to look at them, strange round heads, soft about the eyes. I took her to the beauty parlour once and got her face and nails done. They sharpened up the eyes and lips, quite alluring. She had the bones and the skin, just wouldn't bother. Couldn't believe it. Such a waste. And her hair! Grey quite young, only thirty, a few strands here and there. Have your hair done I said, a nice strong colour you're only young and you don't want to lose the plot yet. Besides, you were meant to be purple. So we did her purple. Everything, pubes and all. (You should do everything. If you go to Surface Domes for a holiday you don't want to be mismatched. I was planning to take her there, but it never turned out.) After this beauty parlour visit I caught her at the mirror trying to scrub everything off. You can't, of course. Silly little trop didn't know. So old-fashioned she thought she could move newface with cleanser, and when that didn't work she bought 100 mls of water. Water! To clean her skin! So expensive and such a waste, and of course after that we couldn't risk tasting the stuff. I nearly cried. She shaved her head to get rid of the purple. That was the last time I spent any real money on her. She just didn't appreciate it.

I've just caught her again – accident, really. You know how rare it is to meet people on those lower levels. I avoid them if I can, rather dangerous in spite of the safety regs. She was down there carrying a bag. Carrying it! Hadn't seen anyone carrying anything for years, not since they set up Autosend. A big bag, like that one in the museum, with handles. She showed me what was in it. Well, I threatened her a little – she never would have shown me otherwise. I mean, I had to know. She might have been working as an over-grounder. I couldn't risk it. Imagine the scandal!

Do you know what she had in that bag? Dirt. Earth. And I'd put my hand in! I was terrified! I was wearing gloves, of course, but you can never be sure. She said she got if from Decontam, passed as safe, but you never know. My gloves might have had a pinprick puncture! I just about died of fright I can tell you.

She laughed, the little witch! Laughed! And thrust her ungloved hand into the bag, pulled out a handful of the stuff. If it hadn't been so expensive I think she would have thrown it at me. Ugh. It gave me nightmares. Whatever for, I asked? Why take such risk?

To grow seeds she said. From above. Look Adriana, she said, real seeds. Real seeds. And her eyes went soft and round like her silly children's. The seeds were taped on to a black piece of paper, so small that they were hard to see, three round yellow seeds. What are they? I asked her. What do they grow? Love apples she said. They don't always work, but I've got three, so one at least should make it. Oh, Adriana, just imagine, growing something you can eat! And her face lit up like she'd sucked pyrotab.

I asked her where she got them. A man, she said. Where? I asked. He was just there, she said, by my bed. I woke up and there he was. This was heartening! She was less narrow than I thought. Don't look like that, she said. I don't know who he was. Even better, I said. No, you don't understand Adriana, he just appeared. The tunnel was locked. He was just there, by my bed in the middle of the night. Well, I couldn't help smirking. She was really making an effort, tears in her eyes and all. So why did he give you this? I asked. Payment? Not at all, she said, no, not that. Never. I don't know why he gave it to me. But I've wanted to grow something for so long. For so long.

Little fool. Silly little fool. It's about time she accepted reality. Seeds and a bag of dirt! But like I said, she's harmless. I think.

And the earth brought forth grass …

one white daisy
pushes bright leaf
grows just dandy
in the crack of crumbling concrete
where a kind man spat.

THE OBSCURING FOG

Harvey Schiller

Skin

Nic Rowan

The curtains are tongues of fire, pouring acrid black smoke. Flames surround him. And all the while there's the crying, the calling from another room, never the room he's in. He stumbles from door to door, calling back, calling out. The low horizon of smoke chokes back his words, dries them in his throat. Now he's on all fours, crawling, while ash rains down. It's raining soft ash and the smell of burning flesh in his daughter's house.

When the dream gets too bad and his pulse sets off the monitor they increase the morphine and he sinks back into stillness.

This man called Andrew, this man sliding through Morphia's arms, clutching and calling, slipping down and further down, this man had a skin licked at by fire, savoured by its tongue, nibbled and sucked and devoured until he was naked as an embryo.

He floats in an ocean of drugs while a clear plastic tube with fine radiolucent fibres explores his lungs and pumps oxygen into him, in and out, in and out. He cannot swallow because of the tube, cannot swallow the smoke and ash that still hovers about his head. Cannot swallow the taste of his daughter burning – or is that his own flesh, still sizzling under the bone, down deep where even the morphine cannot reach?

When they take him to theatre he sinks down into muscle relaxants and drugs of amnesia and in that absence, in that empty space, he dreams of cray boats out at sea, of water deep and cold and blue like gelatine, like crushed ice.

His daughter is there, swimming, swimming toward him, and her unborn children are in her hair, nested in her wild net of hair. She swims up to him and breaks the ice-blue ocean surface. Her skin is coming away from her face like papier-mâché left too long, too wet.

She is becoming pulp in the water. He is a fisherman at sea, casting his line and dragging in only seaweed and papier-mâché.

He rises to the surface of dreams and drugs and sleep and all the graceless places in between. He rises and falls, between earth and sky, between wakefulness and drugged oblivion. He rises and falls over and over again.

Without his skin he has passage to other places, slipping past jail bars lubricated with his own blood. There are dragons and witches, things of stone and breathing wood. He travels long and dark roads that blow dust into the sunset and never end. He travels the roads of his youth and his old age and his death and they are all the same twisted road. Time is there, the threads of his life hanging charred in her hands. Time is weaving the threads back together in a rope made of skin. Time will not stop.

This man with no skin, with nothing to contain him, leaks his fluids straight from muscle, from tendon, his own lymph pouring out in a river to soak bandage and sheet, and sometimes his bed floats in it, floats down to the sea where he sinks and surfaces and sometimes there are boats, and men pulling up strings of pots filled with clacking crayfish. He swims off the bed to free them before anyone realises, before the emptiness is discovered. Sometimes he surfaces from the sea of morphine, at night, to the sound of machines and clicks and whirrs and the impossible task of reclothing himself.

While he lies rising and falling in his bed, what is left of his skin tightens and shrinks around his limbs like so many blackened tourniquets, cutting off the blood, squeezing and killing muscle and nerve and artery and vein. A surgeon takes up a scalpel and slices him open from groin to ankle, shoulder to wrist, flays him open. Then his feet and hands can breathe their blood again.

When his hands and feet are properly breathing he dives deep into morphine again as the surgeon shaves the tiny bits of skin that were left whole, the soles of his feet and the tender, pale insides of his thighs, shaves off wafer-thin parchment layers of skin and lays them down where there is none, so that they can grow roots and turn pink and cover his bare muscle and bone, his nakedness that should never have seen light. He is anointed with silver sulphadiazine and his new skin grows warm. He is anointed with drugs and powders and unguents. He stops leaking. He is contained. His blood rests inside his body.

His daughter comes to him now, bone glittering when she cries out his name, her eyes dried up and rolling loose in their sockets, the stink of burning flesh on her, faint crackle and pop as the fat under her skin roasts away. *Daddy*, she calls. *Daddy*. But no matter what he does she is consumed. She comes to him again and again, an awful phoenix even more naked than him, rising and rising out of smouldering ash.

If he could he would take his newly grown skin, his thin, new skin, peel it off himself and lay it on his daughter's back. He would clothe her in his skin and warm her from her cold metal bed. He would pour fragrant oil on the charred muscle and bone and breathe life into it again, breathe his only daughter upright and revealed. He would.

Rangoon Road

Carol Lefevre

The roads are named after places in India: Bombay, Calcutta, Delhi, Madras, and then the long dogleg of Rangoon Road, as if these places are all the same deal, as if the namer never had a handle on the fact that Rangoon is actually in Burma. People roll their eyes when I talk like this. But that's another thing they never get a handle on – the life-or-death need some people have for beauty, or at the very least a certain symmetry. Over time the population has reduced to a stew of immigrants, the long-term unemployed, deserted women and various lost souls. Vietnamese families three- and four-generations wide squeeze into yellow brick houses, and the old ones still startle on their sleeping mats when the helicopter ferrying emergency cases into Flinders Hospital swoops low over their rooftops. The Viets arrived decades ago. Bewildered and whisker-thin, but quick to fasten on any shred of hope and make something of it, they've flourished. Everyone hates them.

Wherever you look there is a woman with a child on her hip. How did a girl from a middle-class home end up on Rangoon Road? I tell people the route was via the back roads of jazz, the erratic un-brilliant career of songstress Sally Flowers. After that, they don't usually ask any more questions.

The days begin and end with shouting, the women or the kids, or both. It's hard to keep track. On top of shouting there's crying, such a lot of crying around here. Before Christmas especially, the women take on a strung-out hunted look. It's the bloody television. I wish to hell someone would organise a media blackout, because kids would never miss what they didn't know about.

Tonight my next-door neighbour Montsy talks to me through the fence; she asks if I'm buying Batman for Sam this Christmas.

'I don't know,' I say, and I don't.

The pram squeaks as she rocks the baby.

'You got the other kids to sleep?' I ask, to change the subject.

'Si, they-har-sleeping,' Montsy says carefully, and sighs.

'Nice and quiet then.' I wait while she absorbs it.

'Si, perfecto.'

We have these slow chats through the fence a couple of times a week, both aching for adult conversation. It's too bad our language difficulties put us back where we've been all day, talking like children.

On Calcutta, louts are throwing bottles at the Vietnamese whose house backs onto Montserrat's garden. There's no counting how many new panes of glass have been fitted since they moved there. I hear the pram creak and the screen-door snap shut as Montsy locks up.

'*Hasta luego*, Sally,' she calls.

The Viets are fighting back. There's shouting, and a siren in the distance. By the time the law arrives there'll be nothing to see but a mulch of broken glass over the Chinese vegetables.

It's two days before Christmas and I have no money, not a cent. I'm waiting for a pension cheque, two hundred dollars to do the whole festive season. I queue outside the bank, the sun thumping my shoulders as I shuffle forwards and punch in my numbers. Then, instead of cash, the machine spits out a balance slip that claims a five-thousand-dollar debit. I gape at it, while the queue huffs impatiently at my back. Some bludger has hit the wrong button on a computer keyboard and wiped out our Christmas.

Fifty phone calls later I'm no richer and the pension office is closed. Outside the bank, I sink onto a concrete flowerbed and rehearse my speech.

'That's it kids, there is no Father Christmas this year, okay, because there's just no money. I mean *none*.'

The kids are used to hardship, but no Father Christmas! I've always managed to fling myself between them and disaster on this scale.

At home I lie on the floor in the lounge where it's cool and consider potential sources of cash. Fathers two and three have faded to black in the last few months. Oh, they'll turn up sometime, but they won't bring money. Number one is fifteen minutes away by car, if I had petrol to waste.

As I light a cigarette, the blood sings in my veins: *hopeless hopeless hopeless*.

Tomorrow is Christmas Eve. I wake half a dozen times in the night wondering why I feel like shit and then remember. Outside the window, carnations dark as dried blood cast a musky scent over the garden. Eventually, light seeps through the curtains and then, over a mug of coffee, a memory surfaces of more affluent days when I had an account at Harris Scarfe. For all I know, it may still be open. Among a jumble of bills, I find an ancient statement showing a thirty-dollar credit.

'That's correct madam, just pop into the store and we'll give you a current card.'

Yes!' I cry, wild-eyed, jubilant. The bastards can't grind down Sally Flowers.

Harris Scarfe is not the store I would choose for Christmas shopping, but it's that or nothing. With a little over half an hour left before closing time, I career from one department to the next gathering presents; a hairdryer and jeans for Jessie, a flower press and Barbie doll for Maeve, Batman pyjamas and a telescope for Sam – expensive but he'll love it.

The cashier smiles and my blood sings: *how much how much how much*, but I slap the card into her palm and she hands me cash back with the receipt. I'll work out how to pay for it all later. Everything is assembled right down to the wrapping paper, but as I load it into the car it somehow occurs to me that I've left my purse somewhere. I check the bags in the boot, then gallop through the mall, past shopfronts where girls with tinsel in their hair are lowering metal roller doors.

Of course, the purse is nowhere, and the precious cash is *gone gone gone*.

Christmas Day dawns hot, with a scent of eucalyptus and the watering smell from the bed of cosmos flowers the children damped down for me last night. I wake to the rustle of paper, whispers and giggles, and reach for a cigarette. Where will I find money on Christmas Day for smokes? My veins shrink at the prospect of withdrawal. Nicotine is all that keeps me going. Down the hall the hairdryer whines into life, but inside my head there is this louder throbbing: *only two left only two …*

Reuben Grey is the father of my eldest daughter, Jessie. Once we were so close we almost inhabited the same skin. But just as I was discovering maternal love, Reuben was discovering the thrill of heroin and we were doomed. Since then we have fought and made up, fought some more and then made up, because of Jessie, and because we need each other for work. Reuben is not young anymore, and growing frail with abuse, but in his ramshackle way he is always there for us, even if when disaster looms the most he can do is rage that yes, life's definitely a bitch.

Watching the drifting smoke, I know that Reuben will spend Christmas Day playing dead, as he spends so many others. I fling back the covers and decide to gather up the children and Reuben and drive to my parents for Christmas lunch. The parents will hate having Reuben, but he could do with a meal, Jessie could do with seeing him, and I'm dying for adult conversation, even if a lot of the time Reuben talks and behaves just like a child.

Things are going fine; Reuben did a gig last night so he's in funds. We fill the car with petrol, the sun is shining, the kids are singing, we have iced drinks, presents for everyone and enough cigarettes. We've got a booking for New Year's Eve, three-hundred-and-fifty bucks each. Then we'll be through the worst of the white water and into the calm lagoon of January, where no one has any birthdays, no expensive celebrations to deal with between there and Easter. After that it's Maeve's birthday, but we'll cope when it happens. For now it is enough to have survived Christmas with everyone intact. The kids are giggling with relief because it's a long time since they've seen me and Reuben this relaxed, and we bump along the highway with the windows down and the sun beating on our elbows.

My mother freaks out when she sets eyes on Reuben. To be fair, it isn't his fault. Anything can set her off. This time she throws the complete works and disappears into her bedroom. I try to distract the children.

'Lambkins, there are ducks on the lake down the back.'

I raid the bread bin and press stale crusts into their hands. Jessie pulls open the kitchen door and nudges the younger ones out ahead of her. She's wearing one of my old baggy T-shirts to hide her budding breasts, and she throws an anxious glance back over her shoulder as Maeve and Sam, dropping crusts, rush away down the garden.

Ah, Jessie.

When I was her age we lived in another house, not new like this one, which is all smoked glass and sliding doors. It was built of limestone and brick with thick walls, deep sills, dark passageways, and fireplaces where potato skins turned to crisp charcoal among the coals. In winter I lived by the fire in my bedroom, toasting bread and crumpets with a long fork, making melted cheese sandwiches in a jaffle iron. The house was the only sure thing in life, for my mother has always been unpredictable. At Jessie's age I too slid from the kitchen with an apprehensive backward glance.

My father has nothing in common with Reuben. Few people have, except a handful of musicians and his drug dealer, but Dad does his best.

'Played any good shows lately?' he asks.

Reuben's reply is muffled, and I wonder whether to interpret but resist. In the silence that follows, Maeve appears, sobbing.

'The mother duck ggg-rabbed a bb-baby and h-held it under the water. It d-drowned!'

'Ducks don't drown,' I say. 'I'm sure it's – where's Sam?'

'He's on the ssss-swing.'

The diversion doesn't work, and Maeve dissolves into my lap: things are not going so well after all.

Once we've eaten lunch, Reuben's composure begins to slip; I recognise the signs.

'When are we going back?' he whispers. 'We're not staying here, are we? We're not sleeping here?'

In the clear coastal light of my parents' house, I watch his desperation mount. My mother remains locked in the bedroom. I can hear her in there slamming wardrobe doors. The sight of Reuben's edgy frame has triggered the litany of complaints I've heard a thousand times.

'You had so much talent, and you've thrown it all *away away away* …'

My mother's blood sings bitter songs. Is this how my own blood learned to undermine me with its whining refrains?

'You're so thin, Sally, even thinner than before. Don't for God's sake ever wear black. Never. You'll look like a witch …'

As a child, my thinness infuriated her. Clothes she bought for me looked wrong; everything she sewed was so much wasted effort. Once, in an explosion of despair, she slammed my head against the wardrobe at the sight of bones that refused to pad out the shoulders of a dress she had slaved over. In the end I learned to sew in self-defence, found a pattern for a smock requiring only two pieces, and cut out ten, twenty, thirty dresses all the same. The plan was to take control of my clothing, and defuse her anger. I sewed a few, but never finished the lot. When they moved from the old house to this one, she found them, twenty-odd dresses cut to fit my scarecrow frame, the yoke and the skirt still waiting after twenty-five years for two neat rows of gathering stitch.

'Look how much good material you *ruined*,' Mum shrieked, flinging pieces of fabric and the yellowed tissue-paper pattern into the air.

Sunlight streamed into the room where she kept her dress materials, all her projects organised down to matching zips and buttons, and none of them ever started. As the coloured scraps fell, dust flew out and hung suspended, old old dust, the dust of my childhood, *ruined ruined ruined* …

In the afternoon, with the washing-up done, the children play monopoly and my father dozes. Reuben is pale and agitated, tapping his toes in a frantic rhythm that scuffs up piles of fluff on the wool carpet. The old hard knot forms in my stomach; there's nothing for it.

'Dad,' I slide down beside his chair and take his hand. He and I have always been conspirators. 'Reuben needs to get back. Can I leave the children? I'll drive him back to town and then …'

He pats my hand; his skin feels cracked and warm.

'Do what you have to, Sal. The kids will be fine. Stay in town and get a bit of a rest if you like. Once you're gone your mother will be okay.' He looks away, embarrassed, and shakes his head. 'She doesn't mean it you know, it's just …'

I squeeze his hand. We've always been lost for words, too, he and I.

Jessie and Maeve are setting up Sam's telescope on the front lawn.

'I'll come back and get you,' I promise, avoiding Jessie's eye.

'We're going to see the comet,' Sam squeals, and Dad is standing by, full of fumbling encouragement. As we back the car out of the driveway, a shadow flits across the front window. From behind the lace curtains of her bedroom my mother watches us leave, and I wonder what malevolent words whistle in her veins as we wave goodbye.

Reuben hunches forward in his seat. From the corner of my eye I watch as beads of sweat trickle; creases like the seams of old wounds stand out on either side of his mouth. He's given his whole life to music and got nothing for it. If he'd studied medicine for as long has he's studied music, he'd be transplanting hearts by now. Instead, his own heart is in doubtful shape. I often think it's because music doesn't last. At least if you paint a picture or write a book you have something solid, but when the music stops Reuben's hands are empty.

'Come on, come on, come *on*,' he slaps the dashboard, willing the car to go faster.

He can't go on this way much longer. Work always drags him back from the brink, and in those precious moments when he plays, he needs nothing else. But as soon as he stops, craving returns. If I could keep him working I could save his life. But just as I was unable to divert my mother's anger all those years ago, I know that saving Reuben is beyond me.

When we reach the city, I drop him outside his dealer's house.

On New Year's Eve, we play a cafe full of noisy young professionals. They are all out for a good time and have no interest in what we're doing. Reuben and I are musical wallpaper, but don't care because we're doing the only thing we are any good at. In Reuben's case it's all he's ever done, and it is way too good for this gig, but beggars can't be choosers. The boss is a letch with a gold tooth that shows when he smiles. He looks me over in a considering way while we set up, and then sends over a drink. I can't wait to get started, to put the buffer of the music between us and the rest of them.

The songs fly from Reuben's fingers with ease, old, beautiful songs that catch in my throat with the symmetry of the chord progressions, the understated heartbreak of the lyrics. After so many years we work without effort, inventing the arrangements as we go, and the sound is sweet and just a little bitter too. Reuben's head is bowed in concentration over his guitar. In the soft cafe light he looks like a child who has been confined to bed with a long and serious illness. Music, with its healing power, has eased some of the lines from his face; he plays now like a young man in love, firing arrows of sound out through the fog of cigarette smoke and conversation.

'For Christ's sake, play something a bit up!'

It's a man in a grey suit with a tie in a mistaken shade of yellow; he leers into my face as I sing.

'Much more of this and we'll all slit our wrists.'

Momentarily, I wonder if that would be a bad thing. Reuben switches to a faster tempo.

At the end of the night the manager rubs against me with his gold smile; he says he owns a castle in Romania. I take the wedge of money and wriggle away to help Reuben pack up. Drunks spill onto the pavement. Someone has vomited by the door and someone else has trodden in it. We climb into a taxi. As we glide through the city's streets I count the cash, and it's a hundred dollars short. *The bastard!*

I give Reuben his three-hundred-and-fifty and absorb the loss, writhing with fury and resignation. In the morning, the man with the gold tooth will be unavailable. He'll be that way every time I ring. I need the money, but I'll have to let it go. Reuben says he'll ring the musos' union in the morning, but in the morning he'll be lost and the missing cash forgotten.

I come home to Rangoon Road and a message on the answerphone from my father asking when I can collect the children. Suddenly I can't wait to get them home. I can forget how much I love my kids until I imagine them gone. Without them I would fall into a bigger hole than the one Reuben is lost in.

As I drive I remember the porous volcano-strewn landscape of the South East where I grew up, a place where the earth's crust is as thin in parts as the slabs of pastry in a vanilla slice. Limestone caves link and thread away into underground labyrinths, where water trickles and the earth moans and the bones of men and creatures, long forgotten, lay sealed in darkness like secret seams of lace. I remember a farmer's horse put its foot in a hole and stumbled, once. The farmer found an opening that fell away into stale dark air; he dropped in a pebble and waited in vain to hear it land. Undeterred, he returned with a load of boulders and poured them in, but still the hole was not filled. Eventually, divers in rubber suits descended by ropes – three-hundred feet below, the farmer's rocks were strewn like so many marbles in a vast and glittering cavern.

Tired as I am, I steer the car along the freeway towards the house where my mother weaves restless dreams, and where my children sleep so lightly that the counterpane barely rises or falls with their breath. Mist like the fine tulle of a bridal veil floats on the lake in the early mornings. And swans glide, trailing broad ripples on the greenish-glass surface of the water, which is cold, even in high summer, and full of swaying black ribbons of weed. Close by is a rugged coastline, and on that side of the house the air is lighter, rinsed with salt spray from the rolling surf. The house of my parents sits midway between these two bodies of water, which are both, in their own ways, treacherous.

On the freeway, I put my foot down and grip the wheel until my knuckles glow. For Jessie and Maeve and Sam I must be careful where I put my feet, must be mindful to avoid the places where the earth's crust is paper-thin and pitted with holes. For who will raise these children if Sally Flowers should slip and fall?

ERVIN

Ed Douglas

This House in Glenalta

Stephen Lawrence

two- or three-storey, mock-Tudor,
under ten years new –

Steep, olive-black gables, designed
for European snow to slide away easily,

peak disdainfully amongst a cage
of scraggy, mocking, Australian gums.

A rectangle of manicured lawn out back,
bordered by a sawtooth of lilly-pilly, diosma;

cascading ground cover of rosemary,
falls away into a terraced embankment.

Straight overhead, from the lip
of a sculpted chimney-pot,

a young magpie snaps away,
making for lower territories.

The city view pressed hazy blue-black,
silver-edged, causes vertigo.

Crush!

Brunette Lenkić

The vines were wearing her mother's old stockings. Grapes plumped the nylon that guarded them from thirsty sparrows impatient for a spurt of sweet liquid. Marina's father, Paolo, loved his garden and the grapes most of all. When stockings failed to protect the crop, he used his pellet gun.

Sparrows were tasty. His wife cooked them in white wine sauce, like rabbit, or else fried them, which he preferred. He couldn't understand why his children refused to eat them. 'Is crunchy, like chips,' he'd taunt them, with one impaled on his fork. '*Ma troppo ossuto*,' he'd say, laughing, while adding matchstick bones and curled feet to a mound on his plate.

Marina's father embarrassed her. Her Australian friends didn't use strips of old clothes to tie tomatoes to stakes, or grapes to trellises or string silver milk-bottle tops together and throw them over fruit trees to frighten birds away with sudden reflections. Her Australian friends bought their fruit from shops. They threw out their old clothes. *They didn't eat sparrows.*

'Chloe, can you come into the editor's office? Bring your notebook.'

The cadet was startled that Fergus McTavish, the wine writer, knew her name. She grabbed her pad. She probably wasn't going to be sacked if she'd been asked to bring that.

She knocked timidly on the open door of the glass office. David Sculthorpe, *The Chronicle*'s editor, barely glanced up but Fergus smiled and indicated the spare seat.

'Thanks for coming,' he said, as if she'd had a choice. 'David and I are discussing the paper's new project. You know about it?'

'The community wine idea? People bringing in their backyard

grapes to be made into wine? Of course,' she said, trying to sound confident. 'Have you thought of a name for it yet?'

'We've been tossing around ideas,' Fergus replied. 'Why? Do you have a suggestion?'

'Well, I was thinking about it yesterday. You could have a play on words like, "The Grape Escape", or something descriptive, like the "Adelaide Wine Project". But really, you need something snappier, don't you? Something that says grapes and energy and work and fun. I thought, "Crush" with an exclamation mark would be good.'

The editor was studying her. Perhaps she'd been too pushy. But in journalism, you had to stand out or stand aside.

'Also, it fits into headlines easily and it's easy to say and remember.'

Sculthorpe turned to the wine writer. 'Fergus, I agree with you. Chloe is the best cadet for this job.'

Marina winced when her dad offered her friends prickly pear fruit. 'No pricks!' he insisted, having cut off the tough outer skin and sharp spines, which could spike the tongue with invisible splinters. She liked the sweet red flesh with its soft seeds but was ashamed that her dad harvested anything, *anything* at all. Especially if it was free.

He'd tell the family they were going for a Sunday drive; if he put buckets in the boot, she and her brothers knew they'd be winding up the Adelaide Hills to go black-berrying. Going 'to the beach' usually meant the seaweed jungles of Port Adelaide, where her father fished for tommy ruff. 'Going for a walk' always ended at the marshy banks of the Torrens, as it wended a laboured course through suburbia. There, they plucked wild fennel for meat dishes or cut the rampant bamboo into stakes for tomatoes, beans, or her mother's beloved dahlias. The boys hacked away happily but Marina always worried they'd be caught doing something illegal.

For the next six weeks, Chloe would be helping Fergus promote the grape project and its main offshoot, a grape-treading competition. They planned profiles, historical pieces, how-to articles (read wine labels, choose wine). She underlined the word 'pictures'. The more stories they had with photos or graphics, the better.

She got lucky with her first assignment. The elderly backyard grower she'd interviewed turned out to be the great-granddaughter of one of the state's pioneer winemakers, Thomas Hardy. She'd told salacious stories about Adelaide society names who'd lived in the leafy eastern suburbs for generations. 'All hearsay,' she'd winked. Chloe used the best, non-defamatory anecdotes in a feature about the origins of the South Australian wine industry.

It prompted nostalgic and pedantic talkback radio callers and letters to the editor ('*I think you'll find that Mr Hardy's wife was his cousin, Johanna, not Anna, as your correspondent suggests ...*'). Sculthorpe had stopped briefly by her desk, saying: 'Good job on the history piece.' The air crackled with his offhand praise.

Gerhard Weiser was reading about the project in the analytical way he read everything. Though English was his third language, he used it carefully and was often disappointed by the sloppy usage in the city's daily newspaper.

'These people are writers,' he huffed. 'They should be using the words with more ...' he searched for the English equivalent to *Genauigkeit*, 'more cleverness.' No, that wasn't it. 'Precision.' He transferred a biscuit crumb from his fingertip to his coffee cup. The house was now even tidier than when his wife had been alive.

Gerhard was a retired chemical engineer, chess devotee and gardener. He parted his full head of white hair whorling to the left, ironed his clothes crisply, and exercised sufficiently so, although his diaphragm and belly met without deferring to a waist, he looked fit. The only thing that detracted from his genteel appearance was that he was of medium height but his feet and hands belonged to a tall man.

This Crush! perturbed him. Each time he saw the exclamation mark he became primed to read about an industrial accident. Besides the punctuation, he worried about the logistics of turning grapes sourced from so many different people into something drinkable. What about the different growing conditions, the differing quality of the fruit? And what if people brought along table grapes instead of wine grapes?

With so many questions, Gerhard thought it rational and prudent to telephone the newspaper. He was put through to a young woman who had no answers but promised to 'get back to him'. When the telephone rang the next day at 11.42 am, Gerhard expected it would be her. No one he knew would ring when he was likely to be preparing lunch.

'Mr Weiser?'

'That is correct,' he replied. 'May I ask who is calling?'

'Oh, sorry. It's Chloe Allanson, from *The Chronicle*. You rang yesterday about Crush! I spoke to the master winemaker who's overseeing the technical part of this project about your questions. He was very interested.'

'Yes. They were good questions,' he said.

'He answered them but some of his explanations just went over my head.'

'Of course.'

Chloe bristled at that 'of course'. However, the winemaker had said that Mr Weiser was asking what many readers were probably wondering.

She'd heard the newsroom jokes about the project being called 'Vinegar!' The literary editor had suggested '*In Vino, Falsum*'. There were rumours about a glut of grapes; coupled with a downturn in wine consumption, a lot of growers, winemakers and vintners were nervous. Apparently it was an open secret that Sculthorpe had cooked up the grape project with some of them. Wine grapes would be substituted for the community hoard and the public would buy back bottles, not of its own *suburban* blends, but its own *commercial* blends, under the label, 'Harlequin'. It was awkward for Chloe to ask Fergus or the editor directly. When she'd tried, they'd suggested that if she was finding the workload too much …

She'd just ignore the office gossip.

'Chloe,' said the picture editor. 'What's happening?'

The photography department was happy with Chloe. Her stories – and their pictures – were going forward in the paper, including a couple of front pages.

'Well, you've probably heard we're running a grape-treading contest. We're calling it, "Do the Stomp". Basically, teams have to squeeze as much juice as they can in two minutes. Heats start next week at Foothills Winery …'

'Good name for it,' someone said.

'Yeah. They're the sponsors,' she said. 'Anyway, the finals will be the following Sunday. If anyone's interested, you could probably get a photo series. You know, teams slipping in the barrels, close-ups of faces strained with exertion, cheering crowds, judges measuring the results, someone pretending to drink the stuff they squeeze.'

'Why pretending?' the picture editor asked.

'I interviewed the Barossa grape-treading champ the other day and he said there's no way he'd drink a mixture of grape juice, blood, sweat and toenails. Even for a dare.'

Everyone laughed.

Gerhard now felt a proprietorial interest in Crush! Since his contact with *The Chronicle*, he'd met the oenologist in charge of the project. Talking one scientist to another had reassured him. Temperature regulation, controlled addition of yeast, fruit supplemented with commercial crops as needed … The worst of the donated fruit – most of it – would be used for a grape-stomping contest.

The following week, he drove to the competition site, parked, then walked the steep driveway to a cleared area in front of storage sheds where large troughs were set on raised platforms. He was pleased when the newspaper girl greeted him.

'Mr Weiser, are you here as a spectator or a participant?'

'Miss Allanson,' he said, bowing slightly, 'I have no desire to crush grapes with my feet but I am interested to watch other people do so.'

Gerhard watched critically. Many teams were approaching the matter without logic. They crushed the fruit so that juice sprayed everywhere. They would laugh, interrupt their rhythm, and the juice would stop flowing. At the end of the time limit, less than 800 ml would be in the measuring jug. Before leaving, Gerhard inspected the troughs. They were about one metre square, he calculated; timber, varnished inside, with a stainless-steel grate covered in coarse mesh. He saw that the key was to keep the grate clear of skins, pulp and stalks while continuing to stomp. Most participants had barely been able to lift their legs towards the end.

He returned the next day. A couple of teams had squeezed nearly 1.3 litres. Still short of the two litres he thought possible. This time, he inspected the troughs before they were emptied. Most contained perhaps another litre of juice that had not trickled down the blocked grate. Inefficient. Gerhard was sure his theory was correct but he needed someone to test it.

Paolo fretted over Joe's bad luck. Why he step on wood with still a nail in it? In thongs? *Che stupido!* Now, no partner. He and Joe were best grape stompers. Everyone know. Paolo not ask much in life: good wife, good job, children respecting. He love garden anna grapes. 'Oo-fa!' he exclaimed irritably.

He kept pointing out to his wife, Sonia, what all the other teams were doing wrong.

'*Basta*, Paolo!' she said finally and turned away. She saw an old man approach her husband.

'Excuse me, sir,' he said, though they both knew which of them was 'sir'. Paolo picked up the accent. 'I have been listening to your ideas. They agree with my own.'

Paolo grunted. Maybe Germans and Italians were friends during war but now …

'I would like to test these ideas but you do not seem to have a partner.'

Paolo looked him up and down. The old man coulda be 70. Maybe he be having heart attack if he doing stomp, stomp. But big foots.

'So, you want be my partner?'

Gerhard was surprised. He did not want to be the man's partner. He did not want to stomp grapes. He wanted other people to stomp grapes according to techniques he wanted to test.

Before he could answer, Paolo said: 'But you too old.'

Too old? *Too old? Hurensohn!*

'I am in good health. I am very fit.'

Paolo obviously did not believe him and enraged him further by doing exaggerated knee-bends, arms outstretched. Gerhard stretched up, leaned over, legs straight, and put his palms flat on the ground. Paolo began jogging on the spot. Gerhard jogged too, but faster. Both men stopped. Each had passed the other's test.

'Okay. You can go wit' me,' Paolo panted. 'Maybe you fill in papers?'

Gerhard registered himself and Paolo Marinetti as a team. He took off his shoes and socks, rolled his trousers up neatly and marched up the steps and into the trough. Paolo bounded up and jumped in. They grabbed each other's shoulders.

'Remember our tempo,' Gerhard said, hoping the word conveyed more to his partner than 'rhythm' had. 'So we start, first you, stomp-stomp-stomp,' he said, 'then clean,' demonstrating a quick sweep with his foot, 'then I stomp-stomp-stomp-clean. Not too fast, just steady.'

A whistle blew, crushing started, people yelled encouragement. Going well, heart pumping. Then, slipping slightly, losing rhythm, legs becoming heavy. Surely this was already more than two minutes? The yelling continued. Finally, the whistle to stop. Gerhard and Paolo watched while their result was measured: 1.45 litres. It was enough to qualify them for the final.

Paolo slapped his partner on the back. 'Like inna wartime,' the Italian was saying. 'We help togedder.' Gerhard noticed his feet were bleeding.

They arranged to meet again before Sunday. As soon as Paolo and Sonia heard that Gerhard was a widower, they insisted he join them for 'tea' that night. Pulling up to their house, he admired the pink geraniums that adorned their front fence and the corn – next year's seed crop – visible above it. When he entered the yard, Gerhard also saw neat plots of tomatoes and three types of lettuce. Parsley grew everywhere.

Before he found the front door, Paolo came out and steered him to the backyard. He was keen to show off his grapes. 'Looking dis one – lady finger,' he said, pointing to a long variety thinning to fingernail shape that Gerhard had not seen before. 'Is really calmeria ma everyone say "lady finger",' and he laughed at both the silliness of the common name and to include Gerhard in his enthusiasm. 'Also look, sultana, red globe, walt'am cross, currants, muscatel.'

'Not riesling?' Gerhard asked, impressed by the neat rows. He could see that Paolo was a devoted gardener, too: generous, fussy, persistent, practical and sometimes ruthless.

'No, we no have wine grapes. Kids no like. My daughter, she like dis one, muscatel, but my wife, she like sultana. You want try?'

Gerhard was also urged to try the last of the figs. Paolo looked for the drop of honey at the base and tested the body of the fruit between his fingers. He twisted one off the tree. 'Adriatic white,' he said, handing it to Gerhard and watching eagerly while he ate. It was sweet and soft enough that the seeds flowed down with the flesh, rather than lodging in his teeth.

'I think this could be the best fig I have ever tasted,' Gerhard said.

'Good, good. Maybe you never try prickle pear?' Paolo asked hopefully.

Gerhard savoured the quality and variety of dishes served at the

Marinetti table. He approved of the fresh ingredients. To be polite he tried the homemade rosé. Not so good. The four children each poured themselves some, diluting it with water. After the meal, the girl helped her mother clear away.

Gerhard began again on stomping strategies.

'Is okay, Gerry,' Paolo said to him, merry with alcohol. 'We be winning wit' you number one big foots.'

'Feet!' he heard the girl call from the kitchen.

The 'Do the Stomp' final had been heavily promoted by *The Chronicle* and on radio but even the organisers were surprised at how quickly both the winery car park and extra parking arranged at an adjoining oval had filled. Though clouds sulked over Black Hill, rain was unlikely. Spectators sipped wine from tasting beakers and were entertained by a bush band in the lead-up. Eventually, the six teams competing for the title were introduced. They entered the troughs and buckets of grapes were tipped in. When the whistle blew, Marina couldn't believe the enthusiasm.

The crowd was clapping, cheering, yelling: 'Go! Go! Go!' Around her, she heard the same jokes the women used to make when her father and uncles crushed grapes. 'I hope they've washed their feet,' or 'any crunchy bits will probably be toenails.' *Wog* jokes – and everyone was laughing. Her mother suddenly grabbed her excitedly. It looked like her dad and his partner might win.

'Go, Dad!' she yelled.

The news editor and picture editor were arguing over the next day's front-page photo. David Sculthorpe arrived to adjudicate.

'Chloe,' he called, 'read out the story you're writing.'

She had to raise her voice. 'German-born retired scientist Gerhard Weiser wanted to test a theory. Italian-born factory worker Paolo Marinetti just wanted to prove he was a good stomper. Together, they nearly crushed the spirits of champion grape-treading duo, Andy Olivieri and Chris Packard ...'

'Enough,' called the editor again. 'This picture, big,' he said, holding up a portrait. There was a dark-haired, middle-aged, tousled man, grinning largely, his arm around the neck of an older man, who looked tired but deeply, deeply satisfied. A parachute of dark juice was visible at the top of the picture, about to splash.

'Your headline is: "The spirit of Crush!" Use a smaller pic of the winners in action – Andy and Chris wasn't it? – lower down. Put Chloe's lead on the front and spill the story to page three with more pics.'

Gerhard was at the Marinetti's again and Paolo was telling a long joke about village winemakers asked to donate a glass of their best red to a community barrel. When the first glass is poured, it is pure water.

'Water from wine, not wine from water,' laughed Gerhard, before wondering whether he was offending the family's religious sensibilities.

'*Si, si, miracolo,* just like Crush wine!' guffawed Paolo. 'You t'ink we not know why is name after Italian clown, Arlecchino?'

PETREL COVE

Ed Douglas

Going, Going ...

Alexandra Weaver

We sat on the rocks, our hair shifting in the breeze, observing everything in the distant manner of those who will soon be gone.

'If there was one thing you could take,' she said, 'what would it be?'

'One thing?'

'You know, something from here.' A wave broke.

'No idea,' I said. 'Nope. No idea. Maybe nothing.'

'Nothing?'

'You know, I feel as though it's in me, anyway. All the heat. The hills, the mall. Mitcham.'

Apparently this was not an adequate response. For the next hour she returned to the question, putting it to me during conversations about the kind of lives we could expect as career women, women sustained by the giddy endorsement of a graduation ceremony.

'*Think*,' she said, eyes urging it. 'There must be something.'

It was a strange fixation, and one I grew tired of. In the end, I said, 'Port Willunga,' just so she'd stop. She nodded, pleased.

We'd been down there a long time ago – as kids, really, though we'd thought ourselves adolescents, already burdened by and wary of the world. We'd rolled our eyes at boys learning to surf in the shallows, later recounting the moment's details from our bunk beds. Back again every summer, the need to flee the city shifting – simple respite from the heat turning to an escape from our parents, from boys' misplaced affections or fumbling desperation. Then, waiting for exam results, we went with our friends, drinking wine and running along the beach at midnight, thrilled by the lacy tide that caught our feet.

Emily and I decided to go straight to university.

'We'll see everything later,' she said. 'When we've got money, and months free to live it up.' We dreamed about Paris and its boulevards, waking up in an apartment overlooking l'Arc de Triomphe and wandering great gallery halls while snow fell outside. Cards came from friends backpacking through South America, Vietnam, Norway. I stuck them above my desk.

We took summer holiday jobs and kept them through the drizzle and wind of winter, comparing notes on Sunday afternoons at a cafe in the city. I worked at our local video store; Emily waitressed at a coffee shop, a job she despised but never quit.

'I always spill things,' she told me. 'The other day I dropped a pie, and my boss just looked at me, like, *you're an idiot.*'

'I hate him,' I said, leaning in. I hated him for her, and I hoped it helped.

We talked about how she'd soon leave, about elderly customers who'd come in and speak with her about their grandchildren and keepsakes. One carried these treasures around, opening her purse one day to reveal a glittering pocket of jewels.

'I sat down and she set them out,' Emily said. 'She'd been writing her will. It was all organised, and I thought about how strange it was. The end of your life –'

She stopped. I knew.

It was always hard to step back out into the darkening alleys and go home, abandoning the laughter and conspiracy of our hours together. Colour seemed to drain from the suburbs as my little car puttered down Unley Road, shadowy banners strung above the street flapping over traffic. There was something unsettling about them: the exclamation marks and promises of fun for everyone seemed entirely removed from the lives we led, complicated as they were by the nuances of friendship and our own grasping for what was to come, its indefinite shape already suffused with our pledges to be happy and glamorous. Glamour, Emily insisted, was always linked in one way or another to happiness. I still don't really understand.

'You can get away with a lot when you're beautiful,' she told me, and set about making herself so, adopting a routine of facials and monthly bikini waxes, scheduling appointments for acrylic nails and cosmetic dentistry.

'Isn't that tiring?' I said one day, lying on her bed while she plucked her eyebrows, working at them with a stencil that had come free in *Cosmopolitan*. She held the paper still, each stroke completed with mesmerising resolve.

'Not when it makes such a difference,' she eventually replied.

And it worked – a few months later, she began seeing Nick. He was an electrician who asked her out at work one afternoon, creating a story I heard repeatedly: there was a version for day, cool and nonchalant, and one for night, when she'd confess her belief that it might be fate. Emily's mother maintained a feeling for Nick that was somewhere between intense dislike and perplexed curiosity. She would complain to me of his faults: he did not stand up when greeting people; he wore a hat inside; stubs of his cigarettes were sometimes found around the garden, posing a danger to Dexter, the family dog.

To Emily's mind, the more vehemently a boyfriend was rejected, the closer he came to fulfilling the idea she preserved of a misunderstood, roguish man whom she'd love and redeem.

'I love him, Mum hates him – it's perfect,' she would say. I told her this was stupid, and she took it as encouragement.

The men I knew were mild and far too clear in their intentions; their honesty became a deterrent, requiring caution and an unflinching denial of any advances. There weren't many, and turning them down always felt horribly self-indulgent. I imagined my mother urging me to give each one a chance, and the square grip of her hand on my shoulder as she pushed me forward.

'There's nothing *wrong* with them,' I often said to Emily, trying to work myself out. But I knew nobody found happiness by choosing someone whose only benefit was a lack of clear faults. I wished I would fall in love, despised the fact I longed for it. In the hours before sleep I lay awake considering how it might happen, how it worked for other girls. Did they want less, or were they given more?

Things were made worse by Emily's increasing absences – the nights she'd call a half-hour before our dinner plans and cancel, saying she was still at Nick's house. I always joked about it, laughed it off, believed in her promises to make it up. I felt old.

Sometimes, late at night when we had seen a movie and were walking home, we'd talk about the times she'd disappeared. I'd confess my disappointment, and she'd apologise and try to explain.

'When I'm with him, I can't think properly,' she would say. 'I know that seems insane.'

'Sure, I understand,' I said. Birds rustled in the trees; I looked for stars among the branches.

University was not nearly as exciting as we'd hoped. Before starting, Emily had spoken to me at length of her plans to sleep with a lecturer; on discovering there were no suitable candidates, the whole place took on an air of redundancy. I suppose we came across as entirely superficial, and maybe it's true; I can accept such things now in a way that is easy, generous, as though that person were a younger sister of the woman I claim to have become.

After first semester the more practical demands of university took over, interrupted every few weeks by parties that never lived up to our expectations. The afternoons before these events were always their most exciting part: the way hours dropped away, pulled towards the night ahead, and the knowledge that people dotted around the suburbs would soon be uniting. But once there, in it, my dreams of wild experiences and provocative conversations routinely dispersed – always slowly, and always leaving the same fixed, neutral expression. I worried that someone would come past and say, 'Smile!' and could feel anger prompted by the word already at the back of my throat.

The addition of Nick and his mates to our university circle turned it from a small group of school friends into one of expansive possibilities: he was always running into people at the pub and inviting them to someone's house the next night. Emily and I, not wanting to expose our true status as wide-eyed and sheltered, forced nonchalance, hoped nobody would call us out.

'Anyway,' I said to Emily, 'why wouldn't we want to meet new people?'

'Exactly,' she said, 'this is *it*. Let's be crazy, even if we're faking it at the start.'

There was always a search on for new people, different people, any sign of departure from our lives to that point – though I wondered how we'd know who we were looking for. 'You'll know because you'll be having too much fun to think about it,' Emily said, and I agreed, laughing at her analysis.

And so we went to houses in Firle, Plympton, Semaphore: places with rusted gates and laundry tubs full of ice and Coopers. I met mechanics, engineering students, drummers in bands whose gigs I promised to attend. *I'm so far from home*, I used to think, standing in yards stripped of everything but a barbecue and clothesline, studying the city lights from new angles and calculating taxi fares in my head.

Nick navigated these parties with ease, a born entertainer, always equipped with the right comment. He put songs on that people knew and loved; he found a lighter in his pocket when one had just failed. Emily walked at his side, included in the theatrics and excelling in her supporting role. Once, when she went to the bathroom, I ran into Nick by the esky.

'Kate, Katie,' he said, an arm around my shoulders. 'Having a good time?'

'Of course,' I said. I'd just found my way out of a conversation with a couple of earnest film students who'd been competing with one another to name cinema's most underrated directors.

Nick and I stood there for a moment, losing our balance and laughing, looking out at the crowd and its intricacies. I felt the softness of being one of two, and was embarrassed by how quickly I pretended it was mine. I was free by the time Emily returned from the bathroom; Nick quickly reclaimed her, moving to a dark corner and sliding fingers through the waistband of her jeans. I tried not to stare.

At the end of second semester, Emily decided to hold a celebration at her house – her parents were away, and finishing the first year seemed right to mark: a farewell to university as the bright, new part of life it had so recently been, and a show of our readiness to accept the years ahead with precious, mostly false cynicism.

We planned and planned, choosing music and buying strings of cheap lights that we wound around the posts of her verandah. There was chaos in the afternoon before the party when Emily found the white singlet she'd planned to wear had a lipstick stain; she refuted my alternative suggestions while scrubbing furiously, sighing, and scrubbing again. In the end, it came out with bleach. We'd set aside two hours to dress and apply make-up, and though I'd completed both these tasks within twenty minutes I managed to fuss around for another hour, opening and closing powder compacts and watching, as one may watch television, Emily's preparation. She was still riled up from her time in the laundry.

'Oh, shit,' she said, looking around for a tissue, wiping eye-shadow away. 'It's not right. It's not right.'

'Hey, take it easy,' I said. 'It's only a party. Some people coming over. You look great, even without make-up. It's better –'

'It's fine for you. You don't have to impress anyone.' She started again with the brush.

'I might as well not even try, is that what you mean?' I replied, quiet and slow.

'You're pretty enough that it doesn't matter, that's what I meant. Come on, you know it's true. If I could do less, you know I would. But I've got a standard, and it's set now. It always works if I have enough time.'

I could have told her how ridiculous she sounded, how strange and indulgent the whole business was, but I didn't have the heart. In the manner of all those in slight awe of their friends (and perhaps we always are, when they're good enough), I left it alone.

Outside, music needed to be started, cups stacked, ice broken. I was doing that, heaving the bag down against the bricks, when the first guests arrived. In the bustle of the next hour I did not see Emily emerge from the house; I eventually heard her behind me, reacting to a story about someone's last exam, drawing breath and laughing as the punch line was revealed. Nick stood beside her, wearing jeans with several inches of boxer short poking out: this linked him, in a rather clumsy and obvious way, to the boys we'd once considered dangerous and best avoided. Those symbols – the jeans, hats, cigarettes – seemed to betray the kind of boy who would corrupt and change us; it was almost impossible to tell when this fear had turned into interest and, later, longing.

It was a hot night, one that reminded us of summer's real promise – a night calm and heavy with the scent of wattle, which was blooming in a vacant block next to the house. There was an oversupply of spirits in proportion to the lemonade and cola we'd bought to mix drinks with; the liquor's arresting taste lessened after the first few cups. Time wandered on, marked by dancing, someone's conspicuous vomiting and departure, and particularly by Emily's new feeling for vodka, which she had at first with tonic and then on its own. But we were soon facing a shortage of alcohol, even with the bottles our friends had brought. As it so often is at parties such as ours, a half-hour was spent considering the problem before someone offered a solution.

'Go and get something to drink,' Emily said, pushing money into my hand.

'What do you want?'

She blinked and shook her head, then reached for a corner of the garden furniture to steady herself. 'You choose.'

I looked around. It was a fifteen-minute walk; I needed company, though anyone who might have been able to come was by that stage sitting around on the lawn, waving when I caught their eye and silently conveying their comfort and inability to move.

'Do you need a friend?'

Nick, grinning.

'I do,' I replied, rifling through my bag, glad my red cheeks would not be noticed in the dim backyard light.

Nick bent down to kiss Emily goodbye; I saw her hands close together behind his neck, fingers stretched and awkward as those of a child. He and I walked to the street; I smiled, trying to think of something to say. We passed quiet houses, some lit by a lamp at the doorway, a few with television screens flickering into dark rooms.

'I don't know much about you, Kate,' Nick said.

'You know I'm Emily's friend,' I said, immediately wishing the words away.

'That's not enough,' Nick replied, stepping ahead and then turning back. 'What's your story? Where do you fit?'

Formulating answers to these questions got me to the drive-through. Its colour and attendants seemed odd after fifteen minutes in the shadows; the scene moved about before us, the tasks of everyone at work faintly ridiculous.

'I'm a bit drunk,' I said to Nick.

'Isn't everyone?' he replied, walking towards the fridges and taking beer and cheap wine.

'Em likes this, doesn't she?' he called.

I nodded. 'We like the same thing.'

'Well, that's good. Easy to remember.'

He carried the bottles, and after a few hundred metres, said, 'These are heavy.'

'Sorry, sorry,' I said, trying to take the bag. 'Give them to me.'

'No,' Nick replied, 'let's just stop here.'

In the distance, a car revved and tore off.

'Why do you want to stop?'

'Oh, I'm tired. Weary!' He was laughing. 'Come on, sit down.'

'Is it fun being so good-looking?' I said after a while. Every so often this would happen: I'd ask an audacious question just to see if I could, just to see what it felt like.

'Who you calling good-looking?' Nick asked, leaning in to bump my shoulder. 'It's weird for people to say stuff like that.'

'But you are,' I replied – so desperate and yielding, even after all the times I'd told myself otherwise.

'Well,' Nick said, and I put my hand on the kerb, ready to stand up.

Nick didn't speak. Instead he extended an arm; his fingers brushed my bare knee. My legs came apart a little, and I did not consider drawing them back together. He was suddenly close, closer: he was next to me, palm against my spine, the pressure just short of forceful.

'You should have said something,' he whispered. 'If you liked me.'

'*Like* you.'

'If you like me,' he said. A smile into a kiss, Nick knowing, joking, surely aware it could not have been otherwise. I imagined that power as I considered my own – the contact between us I could assure, moving into place and easing his body to the ground. Then I felt the sharp return of sobriety and wished for more to drink.

The twenty minutes we spent by the side of the road ended when a wheezing van turned into a driveway nearby, headlights illuminating us in their sweep.

'I guess we should keep going,' Nick said. It felt like an attack. What did I want, to roam the streets forever? I admonished myself for that, all the while searching for another plan that could preserve the first's simplicity and somehow negate all that lay ahead.

We opened a bottle of wine and took turns drinking from it as we made our way down the road, around the corner that curved past the creek, and up the hill towards Emily's house. Every few minutes we stopped to get our story straight. It was easy enough to construct: the first place had been closed, and we'd walked on to find one. Easier still was the way we fell together after speaking; I recklessly hoped someone I knew would come past and see us. Still, on the edge of our plan lingered the raw truth that lies would never completely dismiss what had happened – dwelling in that interesting meeting of self-hatred and pride, I asked Nick what he'd do.

'Oh, it was already over,' he said, full of the confidence that had led both Emily and I to him.

'Were you going to break up with her?'

'Yeah,' he said. 'I think she tries a bit too hard.'

'Only to impress you,' I said, dropping his hand. I pushed against his chest. 'She only –' There was nothing to say, and nothing I could manage, not through my tears.

'Oh, shit,' Nick said. 'Don't cry. Come on …'

I let him pull me along, then walked inside the house and wondered who would ask the first question about our absence. Odd how we suspect private changes are at once publicly noticed; when we wandered out the back, people barely looked over. They were singing along to an old ballad, watching the flame from a burnt-down candle cut through the smoky air.

Emily was asleep.

'She drank a *lot*,' a girl named Anna said, walking past us with a blanket. 'She found a cask of red in the cupboard.'

Left alone by Nick, who disappeared almost at once to play his favourite songs and encourage others to dance, I wandered the empty rooms of Emily's house, reassured by the framed paintings and polished furniture, the calendar in the kitchen on which doctor's appointments and dinner parties had been marked.

Emily's bedroom door was ajar; by the hallway light I could make out her form on the bed, neck and shoulders pushed awkwardly against the pillow. Shoes still on, and a hand still within reach of a glass of red, which sat on a nearby chair. Immobile, I watched her breathe. After some time I went in, slipped the shoes off and eased her legs under the covers.

'Hi,' she said. Eyes blank, closing again as soon as she'd found me.

'Go back to sleep,' I replied, and sat by the bed until I was sure she had. I thought about everything we'd tried together to understand, our huddled discussions and the peace created by finding an ally in that process, however melodramatic it all seemed in retrospect. To suddenly become part of the world's complexity was at once bizarre and underwhelming; I realised the plotting and intent we'd always assumed of our betrayers could have been simply a convenience.

The next two years went faster than they should have. That's what we always said: faster than they should have, though I can confess I was privately grateful for the months' speed, for burying myself in essays and test preparation while Emily did the same. I spent both summer breaks working full-time at an office in the city, entering endless streams of data into a system nobody ever seemed to consult. Emily's waitressing progressed to a top-end restaurant: I'd sometimes stop in early on a Friday night, order an entrée and chat with her while she folded napery.

Then it was over: following a flurry of final exams and semester papers, we were finished. A group of us went down to Brighton to drink champagne in a hotel on the esplanade. It was mid-afternoon; we watched grandparents guide children on tricycles along the footpath, barely able to give chase when pedals spun too quickly. Our friends, who'd given assurances of a late, rowdy night, excused themselves as the hours went on – they had dinners to attend, boyfriends to meet. Someone had to pack for a job interview in Canberra.

Emily and I found ourselves alone, wandering outside and down to the rocks. The tide was out.

'I kissed Nick at that party,' I said. 'The one in first year.'

'Did you?' she said, head still.

'Are you surprised?'

A pause. 'The thing is,' she replied, 'isn't it strange how a person can come along. Out of nowhere, you know, and then they're every-thing to you. Just – you can't think straight, you're so worried if they don't ring …'

'Do you miss him?'

'No, not really. It was a million years ago. I suppose it was just the first time I'd felt that awful pull away from everything. Awful because it's so good when you're in it. And you forget about normal life.'

Then I said, 'I'm sorry,' understanding at once how feeble and absurd the word could sound, even after all I'd learnt about its importance.

'Don't worry about it,' Emily replied. The situation, or I, did not deserve more.

So we sat there, held together by the spare threads of a common past, knowing already the way in which we would separate, the dif-ficulties in preserving our friendship.

I thought about Emily's question: *If there was one thing you could take, what would it be?* That interest, that real interest that she had shown in what I wanted. My throat grew tight and dry.

'I'd take it all,' I wanted to say to her. But of course that was not possible, no way anything could be moved or kept. There was only the fixed shape of our youth, its fickle beauty and forced end. Only a trail of days together, and now the exquisite moment of the sun sinking below the horizon. Her face pink in its glow, caught by the ocean's surface.

'It just falls, doesn't it?' I remember her saying once, smiling. 'It's there, and then it's gone.'

Opening Night, West Beach

Cameron Fuller

    Stars arrive early. The last
seconds of sunlight turn
    orange and purple velvet

into pink silk. Lying on sand
    an audience hears the ocean
breathing in the inner shells of minds.

    The sun dissolves in dark oil
as dogs splash and ripple
    and couples pose in silhouettes.

Suddenly on the surface a fin
    then a jab of fear. But it's
all ephemeral. The act

    closes with the villain
uncloaked as a dolphin.
    The scene moves to the slow

erosion of dunes and the glitter
    of city beyond. As meanings
flicker like streetlights on the coast

    a meteor fizzles above to show
there's more to being in a theatre
    than watching a story unfold.

The play does not end with
    trails of nebulous emotion
burning under moonlight. A final

    touch of hot night air on skin –
the curtain drops,
    the spool of love unravels.

In Dreams

Larry Buttrose

The cold remains of Sunday roast lay on the plate in front of me, the sprigs of cauliflower entombed in a sarcophagus of congealed white sauce.

'So what's it about, this test tomorrow?' my father asked.

'Ancient Rome.'

'Big topic. Specifics, please.'

The clock showed five past two. I only had five minutes left. My mother went to take the cold mess from in front of me, but my father's hand stayed her.

'It's on everyday life in Rome.'

'And what was it like,' he asked, 'everyday life in Rome?'

'Hard.'

'I bet it was. Particularly for Roman boys who wouldn't eat the nice Sunday lunch their mothers had cooked.'

I cleared my throat. 'It was slaves, dad.'

'What?'

'Slaves. If you had any money, it was slaves who did the cooking.'

'What's the difference?' my mother said, swiping my plate. 'Wife, slave, what's the difference?'

'What you mean?' my father said.

'How it sounded.'

But then she smiled at him, if a little strangely, and walked off down the hallway. After a final look at me my father followed her. Not wasting a moment, I opened the front door and was off.

I didn't have far to go. A British racing green Mini idled at the corner. The driver dropped the clutch and we zoomed away through the comatose suburban streets.

'I'm Greg.' He took a drag on his Peter Stuyvesant. He was probably no more than eighteen, but to my eyes was a grown man, complete with wispy chin beard and smoking affectations.

'Troy,' I lied.

He smirked at me sceptically. 'Men swear by Troy's Menswear, eh? Well, up to you what we call you.'

I had spoken to him only once, on the telephone, in reply to the handwritten advertisement I'd seen in the coffee lounge on Henley Square.

'What kept you?' he asked.

'Sunday lunch.'

'Cigarette?'

'No thanks.'

He told me he'd driven over from Exeter and that he worked in a garage on Port Road. Despite an abrupt manner he was friendly enough, and his smile was shy. I already knew enough to expect as much in a bass guitarist.

The car radio was on 5KA, Big Jim Slade. A jingle played for Solomons Carpets, and next Big Jim boomed a paean of praise for a new band he said everyone was talking about, the Masters Apprentices, and played their song.

'I love it when the singer does all the rooting grunting,' Greg said. He took the Mini hard through an S-bend. 'Played much electric guitar?'

'A bit,' I lied again.

I had bought my acoustic classical only six weeks before, and had never even touched an electric. My entire repertoire comprised 'The House of the Rising Sun' and 'Honky Tonk Women'.

'Read music?'

'Chords, yeah.'

'Anyone who can read can read chords mate. The dots, I mean.'

'The notes? Not … not yet. Still learning,' I admitted.

'Doesn't matter too much I 'spose,' he said, 'only on rhythm after all.'

We pulled up outside a two-storey cream-brick house on Anzac

Highway and were met at the front door by an overweight man in an open-necked shirt and cardigan, *Sunday Mail* in hand. He looked at us with bored contempt. 'Upstairs, still in bed.'

'Dunno why he boards here with that old queer,' Greg said as we climbed the stairs. 'Must be cheap's all I can say.'

Martin had his own front door at the top of the stairs. Taped to it was a small black and white photograph of Roy Orbison, skin the whitest shade of pale and sunglasses the deepest melancholia of black.

'The Big O,' Greg murmured, with a nod of respect, and knocked on the door.

After a delay of a half-minute it opened, and a girl stood yawning in a faded blue sheet. She was about fifteen, pimply and pasty. Her nails were black and her dyed black hair bunched in tangles.

'We're here to pick up Martin,' Greg said. 'Band practice.'

The girl walked away without a word. As she did, the sheet flapped open and I saw her from neck to ankle, the first naked female body I'd ever seen. If only it had been a front view, I couldn't help but wish.

We followed her and found her back in bed with a sleeping man I took to be Martin. The bed was a stained mattress on a shaggy green carpet strewn with greasy-fingered glass tumblers, an empty whisky bottle and a full ashtray. A skimpy dress, black stockings, bra and panties lay entangled with a man's purple shirt and black jeans. The pockmarked walls were bare except for a poster of Roy Orbison in concert. In the corner was a fire-engine-red Fender Stratocaster, the first I'd ever seen up close.

Greg nudged Martin's shoulder, and his eyes blinked open, murky green. He yawned a bad-toothed grin and sat up to roll himself a cigarette. His dirty blond hair hung in strings around a leathery, tobacco-cured face. There was a tattoo on his bicep, a red heart pierced by three swords. I thought him older than Greg, twenty; twenty-one even. He slipped a hand under the sheet the girl had around her, onto her breast, and she didn't protest or seem to mind.

'So the old chook let you in okay,' Martin said. His voice was surprisingly pleasant, well modulated and articulated, if raspy.

Greg jerked his head in my direction. 'This is Troy, the young guy I mentioned. Rhythm.'

Martin's eyes rested on me. 'Young's the word,' he said with a tweak of his lips.

'I'm fifteen,' I protested, too much.

'Thirteen if that.'

'Okay. I'm fourteen.'

'How long you been playing? Month? Six weeks?'

'Six months.'

'Oooh, sorry,' Martin giggled, 'half a whole year he says.'

The girl had been attempting to affect aloofness, but Martin ended that with a little squeeze of her breast that made her squeal.

'Martin, that bloody well hurt!'

I realised from her accent she was English, a girl from out at Elizabeth perhaps. She ran off into the sad little living room I could see adjoining, pursued by a 'sorry, love'. This time she kept the sheet securely wrapped round her.

She had left Martin lying naked on the mattress, but his only acknowledgement of it was another chuckle. Then he sprang to his feet with an unhinted-at agility and pulled on the black jeans and crumpled shirt.

'Well come on you chaps,' he said, grabbing his guitar and a leather bike jacket from a hook behind the door. 'The muse awaits.'

Frank's family lived in a rambling whitewashed stucco Spanish villa on the seafront at Grange. It was on a deep block, and there was a tin shed down the back he was allowed to use for band practice on Sunday afternoons.

Frank was younger than Martin and Greg, sixteen or so, but was in many respects as self-possessed as Martin. His father was a real estate agent and Frank went to a private school up in town. I guessed he'd go on to university, do law, even architecture. He was good-looking, with an easygoing manner. His limbs were long, his finely-featured face framed by the dark hair he fringe-flicked from his eyes. I couldn't work out why he was only the drummer: he was easily good-looking enough to be the singer, more so, truth be told, than Martin, and I subtly intimated as much.

'Funny that,' Frank said as he led me into the freezing, half-lit shed. 'But there's only room for one Adolf in every band, and one bloody poet too, so we just have to put up with him. He's all right actually, as far as it goes.'

The band set-up looked like a pagan ritual scene. The drums occupied centre stage, flanked by amplifiers blinking with little red lights and emitting a low expectant buzz. Out front microphones stood on stands, frayed leads running away. Frank took an electric guitar from a battered case, plugged it in and tuned it.

'I started out with this,' he said, then nodded towards the drums, 'before I got to those.'

'You prefer drums?'

'In rock, drums are it. The rest's window dressing.'

He handed the guitar to me. After my acoustic it felt like a chunk of scrap metal. 'Played an electric much?' His grin made the question rhetorical. 'Give it a go. Let 'er rip.'

I made an open C chord, and dragged the plectrum across the strings. Sound exploded from the speaker behind me, and ricocheted around the ceiling of the tin shed. I was astonished at the instant power I possessed.

'Nice, eh? Play bar chords?'

'Er, not yet.'

'No worries, you're only on rhythm.' He looked around. 'Now where have those two bastards got to?'

We went outside. Big Norfolk pines lined Seaview Road behind the house, making it shadowy between the shed and the back fence. I could hear the wind through the treetops, and the waves lapping the beach on the far side of the house. The sea smell prickled my nostrils. Every inch of the old place looked salt-encrusted, even the windows, and paint was peeling everywhere. Frank appeared to read my thoughts. 'Gives the old man nightmares keeping up this dump.'

Martin and Greg were huddled in a corner against the back fence. 'Smoke?' Martin asked me.

'No thanks. I don't.'

'Not even a little joint?'

I had seen pot smoked on television, in silly melodramas where people ended up shrieking in straightjackets, and TV current affairs segments with reporters poking microphones at giggling uni students at parties, but this was the first time I'd ever been offered it. I hated cigarette smoking, but was tempted to this out of curiosity. There was the complication too that it might be a 'peace pipe': that if I wanted to be one of the boys, I'd better smoke with them. But an image flashed into my head, of my mother crying as I phoned her from the police cells to say I'd been arrested on a drugs charge, and I too clearly saw the defeated look on my father's face in a courtroom.

The joint hung there, smouldering between Martin's nicotine-yellowed forefinger and thumb. 'Well?'

'No thanks, not before I play.'

He raised an eyebrow and slipped the joint back between his lips. 'Ah, the dedicated musician.' He exhaled a billow of smoke and passed the joint on to Greg, who clenched his teeth and dragged hard. Frank didn't take his turn. Perhaps he worried about his parents too. 'Some artists say it helps them create,' Martin went on. 'Hendrix. Baudelaire used all kinds of stuff.'

'Oh,' I said. I of course knew all about Hendrix, but who was this Baudelaire?

'You're probably wondering who Baudelaire plays with,' Martin laughed.

'Oh come on Martin,' Frank put in, 'stop playing the big know-it-all. Who cares if you happen to know the name of some old French poet, *Flowers of Evil,* big deal.'

'Ooh, so we are in a perfectly shitty little mood again today are we, Frank?' Martin taunted.

The silence that followed was broken by Greg coughing as he handed the joint back to Martin.

'So what's the name of this band?' I asked.

'We don't have one yet,' Frank said. 'This is only our third practice.'

'At last count there were three candidates,' Martin said, 'The Handsome Crabs, The Worry Beads, Cat Scratch. What do you think?'

'Well ...' I replied.

'I sense doubt. Any ideas of your own?' Martin paused, waiting for a reply from me. 'Any ideas at all? Or is that too big an ask?'

'Oh come on, let's just start,' Frank said. He moved off towards the shed, but Martin didn't budge.

'What did you say, Frank?'

'I said let's start.'

Martin stared at him. 'When I'm ready. That's when we'll start, mate. Okay?'

The two gave each other a look, and Greg couldn't help laughing, nervously. Martin ground the stub of the joint beneath his Cuban heel and went inside, followed in order by Frank, Greg and myself.

Martin picked up his guitar and plugged it in before standing quietly with it. He looked good with a guitar, I thought. It was the way he held it. There was something about how all the greats held their guitar, I realised: Elvis, John Lennon, Pete Townshend, Hendrix. It was like a physical extension of them, but it was more than that. It was as if they had been born to hold their guitar just like that, in their own way: Elvis caressed its curves, Lennon thrust it out rebelliously, Townshend did his big mad roundarm strums before smashing it against an amp, Hendrix writhed erotically with it on the floor, wrestling it, the strings between his teeth.

'So what do we start with?' Martin said in my direction. 'How about "Stone Free"?'

This was the latest Jimi Hendrix Experience song on the hit parade. It was a Power Play on 5AD and you heard it about fifty times a day. It was an explosion of raw guitar energy, of shimmering reds and purples and blues, of pure power, Hendrix, inimitable.

'Pretty big one, first up.'

Martin smirked. 'Too hard, yeah, you're right. How about "The House of the Rising Sun"? You must know that, it's Lesson One in all the Teach Yourself Guitar books.'

Despite the paternal sarcasm, I breathed relief.

Martin started up, finger-picking the first bars, a chill emanating from the Fender. I noticed then the little hand-lettered price-tag that dangled from it: $25.00, from Laurie Tredrea's, the pawnbroker. Perhaps Martin left it on as some sort of inverted pride. I wondered too how the guitar had made it to a pawnbroker in the first place, and about the sorry muso at the end of some long, awful road. What was left of you after you hocked your Fender?

The drums and bass kicked in. I picked my moment to come in on the rhythm, and a moment or two later Martin looked over and gave me an almost imperceptible nod. I gave an equally minimal response, and we swung into it, pretty ragged, but all things considered, not too bad.

Then Martin began to sing, and I knew instantly why he was the leader of the band. His voice was a deep blue lament, a wonder. You could have listened to that voice all night, the texture, the tone, yet astonishingly it belonged to such a conceited prick.

We got past the first verse, and the band started cooking. I realised the origin of the term then. All the ingredients get tossed in, perhaps not so appetising in themselves but given the right amount of heat they meld in an alchemical miracle, much richer and sweeter than the sum of the parts.

'Oh, Jesus wept!' Martin yelled out suddenly, stopped playing and tossed his guitar aside. Before anyone realised what was happening he was up beside the bass drum dragging a startled Frank up off his stool by the lapels of his denim jacket.

'Listen you idiot, how long do I have to put up with your utter lack of rhythm! I mean, how do you dance, man? How do you fuck for Chrissakes!' Still holding Frank, he gestured towards me. 'See him, this kid the dog dragged in … even he's got more talent than you! A shithouse door banging in the wind's got more!'

Frank broke the hold. 'Yeah? Well no one, no one's more up themselves than you are, dickhead! Talk about ego!'

'Yeah, well maybe I am! An arsehole you all think, and you're probably right! But I can do my job. When it comes down to it I can sing and I can play. But you can't … you're useless! The only thing you bring to the group is this shed!'

'Get fucked,' Frank said, if quietly.

'No, you, you get fucked! Go and get utterly fucked! For the first time ever no doubt – do you good, wouldn't it! So yeah, you go and get yourself fucked, Frank.'

In the ensuing silence I had no idea how we could go anywhere from here. The room felt even colder, and I realised the late winter sun was going down. Dark soon, I'd be expected home.

Greg spoke up. 'Well, I'd do that, yeah, get utterly fucked. Trouble is, got no volunteers, have I.'

Despite themselves, the other two couldn't help smiling. 'Jesus you're a case, know that Greg?' Martin said, before erupting in a peal of laughter. A half second later Frank joined in, and Greg, and I was too, laughing with relief, deliriously, at the madness of being here with these three strangers making music in this frozen tin shed by the sea.

The four of us walked towards each other and laughed, arms around each other's shoulders, turning round and round in a little wheel until we felt dizzy. This is what it is to be an artist, I thought, the silly arguments and the insanity, and the little pin-pricks of something magical just when all seems lost. This is why I answered the ad in the coffee lounge, why I made the call and am here today, and why there's no turning back now. I am one of these lunatics.

The laughter subsided, leaving the four of us standing there.

'Well, so?' Martin said, tears of mirth still in his eyes. 'Suggestions, come on.'

'How about "In Dreams",' Frank said, and I sensed as he did that he had been summoning up the courage to say it.

'What …?' Greg said, 'Jesus no, Frank, not again.'

'Frank,' Martin replied, still smiling, 'you know we can't do that song, mate.'

'Why not?'

'Because like I keep on telling you, no one can sing it. It's like our young friend here said about Hendrix. I can't sing that song, not "In Dreams". It's impossible.'

'I'm not suggesting you sing it. I want to.'

'What?' Martin said. 'You? You want to sing "In Dreams"?'

'Yeah. Me. I do. I've got the sheet music here.'

Frank passed around photostat copies. His face was flushed, his hand trembled slightly. Martin gazed down at the face in dark glasses on the cover of the sheet music.

'It's easy enough to play,' Frank prompted.

'Of course it's easy to play. But it's not possible to sing. You don't just have a crack at his songs … they're special. Art.' With a flick Martin opened the sheet and ran his forefinger down until he reached the final verse. 'See this Frank, this mark, under the last line of the song, "Only in dreams in beautiful dreams"? See the "O" printed there, under the word "Only"?'

'Yeah. So what?'

'That is there because there is only one person who can sing that big top note. Only one. Roy Orbison.'

'Bullshit,' Frank stated.

'No, not bullshit, my friend.'

'It has to be.'

'Why? Why do you say that? Are you calling me a liar?' Martin said, renewed threat entering his voice.

'What, you expect me to believe that nowhere, in the whole world … that there's no one who can sing that note like Roy

Orbison does?'

'Yeah, that's what I expect you to believe. That's what I'm telling you, Frank. And you better believe it. If you intend to remain a member of this band, that is.'

'What?' Frank protested, looking towards me for support. 'You can't be serious. I mean, you expect that just because you think Roy Orbison is the next best thing to Jesus Christ, everyone else has to agree? Who do you think you are Martin, some new bloody messiah?'

'No, just the leader of the group. And I'm not going to allow this band to waste its time trying to learn a song we can't do. Not do properly anyway, not that would do it justice, him justice.'

'Him meaning Roy Jesus Fucking Christ Orbison,' Frank smirked.

Martin did not hesitate. I saw his fist shoot out and disappear into Frank's stomach, saw Frank's eyes widen, heard his low 'oof'. He fell back, doubled over, and looked up, shocked.

'You're fucking mad!' he got out between gasps.

'You're ignorant. Shut up.'

'You shut up, arsehole!'

Martin took a step towards him.

'Get out, just get out,' Frank yelled, retreating a pace.

'What?' Greg said quietly. 'No …'

Frank turned towards Greg, and we could all see the hurt in Frank's eyes then, not so much from Martin's blow, but at having to pursue the course he had stumbled onto.

'Piss off, all of you. Get out.'

'Oh, so we're taking our cricket bat and going home are we?' Martin said. 'What else could you expect from the son of a real estate agent? You can't rock and roll. You could never rock and roll. It's from the dark side of the tracks, the shacks.' He picked up his guitar and jacket and walked out.

'Hey, Martin!' Greg called.

The gate onto the street creaked open and clanked shut.

'Christ,' Greg sighed, 'why does it always have to be like this?'

'What?' I asked.

'Everything, like this, always,' Greg said, and ran off after Martin.

In the quiet after they had gone I realised Frank was crying, softly. I couldn't bear it, and went to put a consoling arm around him, but he shrugged it off.

'What are you, pooftah?'

'Frank ...'

'Piss off. Just piss off.'

He walked away. I heard his feet crunching the gravel path back to the house, leaving me alone with the drums and guitars of our nameless band that never was.

'Where've you been!' my father called. My eyes adjusting to the semi-darkness, I saw him in his armchair, cigarette in one hand and beer in the other, and my mother in the matching armchair, cigarette smouldering in her ashtray. The TV news was on, a helicopter lifting off from a paddy field. Scenes on board followed, of a crewcut young soldier blazing away at a half-dozen piglets running through some deserted Asian village.

'Bloody madness,' I muttered.

'What was that?' my father asked.

'Nothing,' I said.

'Where've you been all this time?'

'Studying.'

'Off chasing some bird.'

'Dad, I was studying.'

'Bullshit. And don't you bloody swear.' Then he said, 'Go and pour yourself a beer why don't you. Footy replay's coming on, Torrens and Sturt.'

I went out to the kitchen wondering if I would get any time later on to look over the Roman stuff. I had to do well this year, and the next, and the one after, to get to university, to get out. And I had to do the right thing by my parents too. If I didn't, who would?

I thought of Greg at the garage, and the dream of playing in front of fans, getting girls, getting money, getting out, all misting away to the hard residue of a car in for a service and a wrench in his hand. I wondered what he would do now, and hoped he would try again.

Over the years I came to doubt the strange day of the band ever occurred. The details didn't seem quite right for one thing. Surely by then I had gotten past the Sunday rite of the congealed vegetables? Did I have a guitar then: wasn't that a year or so later?

But the day did happen, in all the crucial detail, down to the *Flowers of Evil*. Indeed, it is only decades later that I am certain of it, after the passage of sufficient time to cross the shadow line from what we prise from the travails of our days into what we prize from our nights, in dreams.

Glenelg Beach

Courtney Black

It was summer after summer with you in my head –
it was sand-riddled arcade pacman dreams all summer
boulevard visions of eating you up like ice-cream
or coming like trams on the beach here close together.
Down by the palindrome shoreline, bending back
curved round at the start & the end and never changing
years pass. The water could tell me that now I look older
but so that it won't tell lies, it tells me nothing.

Here unhappy families bring deep-tanned cagey children
tram ride stopping & starting & barely speaking
those show & tell lies: What I Did In My Summer Holidays

that kid who swelters in her city flat most of the summer
& comes to this beach for a treat. Her tensing parents
wincing the shell-strewn sands & I found something
for primary school show & tell, with more school coming
six & sixteen. All years ago brought together –

the week we first did it, in summer, I came to this beach
juddered my tram ride alone to the palindrome shoreline
laid out in the sands I swear, there you were still on me
with me & near me. Your little-guy milky skin
your smell like milk at the beach with that overtone hint
of orangey mint fresh smoky nightclub jacket.

What I Did In My Summer Holidays. That's just a trap &
they want to hear beach-visit stories & not the rest
it's a test, what you pick up to keep at the palindrome shoreline.

Not needles & punctured-plastic cone-piece bottles
or bottle-brown broken-up glass & cigarette packs.
There's plenty of that sort of thing on the lounge-room table.
The roaring & rattling parents that break up your sleep –
if your nights grow up that way then that's your own secret to keep
what you take in for showing & telling is not the truth
but the shell you picked up, and shone with toothpaste, as proof but

you know how that is. Bent cagey over your putt-putt
little-guy burned neck escaping the high sun raging
& I know that you always knew it now, realising back
as a grown-up, rattling back along the tramline
of memory still at the shore & never changing.

At night in my yellow sheets-ends, gritty with foot-sand
proverbial pillowslip there, where all lost loves are found
again, curving back to the start & never changing

the years we fooled round in. Teenage & low-twenties
these leave-taking pictures reside with me. Lurid tourists –
all of them version of you, parading your sexiness
well, fuck you & your sexiness. Cheeky at eighteen
curving your hands through the sand at the palindrome shoreline
making a sandcastle-woman, complete, neck-to-knees
with a chest curving round & then down to a stomach like mine.
Sly-grinning, avoiding my eyes. You dirty kid
wet-stuck slabs of sand on the back of your tan-line
at Glenelg & I loved you then as now, I did but

so that I wouldn't tell lies, I told you nothing
but took just what I found you & I found something
milky reflection there lingering in the shallows –
then grown-up broke it up, smashed it. Hurt you silent
left & pretended you'd left me. Not even sure now

too proud to tell you & broke you up. Watched you leaving
with her. Me still niggling like sand between your toes

& here's where some strange guy asked me: hey me & my friend
we got a bet on, how old are you? So I told them
the truth then, I told them sixteen. But didn't stick round to
hear out the chat-up punch-line 'cos I was still dreaming
of you with your little-guy waistline. Vulnerable skin
curved round at the start & the end and never changing –
warming me like the juddering seat of the tram
as a grown-up, rattling the tramline coming home.

Zoo-Narmy

Colin Varney

'How long we got to live mate?'

Darryl readjusts his grip on the surfboard. Fixes me with bleary eyes. Some party last night. The tanks of compressed air are dragging off my back. Lift my arm to show I'm not wearing a watch. He grabs it.

'Where'd you lose that? Back seat of Janey Wilton's car? Is that where you were last night, you dog?'

Feel like a husk. Brain shrinking, hangover throbbing. There's a bloke in a dinner suit with snorkel and flippers. A group in full scuba gear. Someone with a long white beard and a sack-like robe: think he's supposed to be Noah. Carnival atmosphere.

Placards: 'SURF'S UP'. 'I'M SHAKEN NOT STIRRED'. 'THE END IS NIGH SO GET HIGH'.

Don Dunstan on the foreshore, surrounded by photographers. Thrusts an open palm towards the waves, Canute-like.

I pull the mouthpiece free. 'People sold their houses. Can you believe that?'

Darryl hoists the board firmly. 'Tell you what, when that baby comes in I'm riding it to wherever it goes. 'Cause if there's sin in this town I want to know where.'

The religious fruitcake said it was coming today. God had stuck a pin in the calendar and it landed on 19 January 1976. Midday. Scoff your lunch quick before the earth trembles and a wall of water cleanses evil from the streets of Adelaide.

Woke up on the floor at Darryl's. Apocalypse bash. Looked like the Four Horsemen had galloped through the lounge. We left his dad to clean up and went to check out the tidal wave. Or as Darryl says, the 'zoo-narmy'.

Strain my eyes towards the horizon. Is it higher? Has it heaved up a notch?

Cast a sideways glance at Darryl. There's a surge of guilt. Best friend since first year high. Sure, there'd been some hiccups. He'd thought Skyhooks were poofy and preferred the tough rockin' blues of The Aztecs. And after he tried to convince me the moon landings were a hoax we didn't talk for a week. Consequently, my essay on *Romeo and Juliet* was rank, as he was a whiz with the bard and usually helped me out.

'What a farce.' He peers around contemptuously. 'This puts the zoo in zoo-narmy.' Beams, pleased with himself.

Struggling with a strange, sad feeling. Akin to nostalgia. As if I'm already missing his friendship. As if he's found out what I did last night and our time together's already a memory. You do weird things when doomsday's due.

Because I know where my watch is. In the bedroom next to Darryl's.

The waves would draw back. Biggest low tide ever. Fish flapping on a stretch of sand that had never been exposed to air before. Sea swelling and building, nudging the horizon higher. Then rumbling in. Vibration in the sand, thunder in the air. God's growl of vengeance. The Old Testament was right about Him. The wall of water smashing into the beach, snatching Darryl and I up into its whorl. Lifting us helplessly and carrying us deep into the suburbs. A sin-seeking wave. Plunging us past the Glenelg cinemas where I'd covertly held Darryl's sister's hand during *Conquest of the Planet of the Apes*. Trying to summon enough courage to go the grope. Only to catch Darryl's glare of disapproval. The wave turns, whooshing us over the rooftops of my neighbourhood. The maelstrom forces us down and tumbles us for a moment before my lounge-room window. There's the spot in front of the telly where I wanked during *Number 96*.

Snatched up again. I thrust the mouthpiece at Darryl and we buddy-breathe, eyes wide in terror. We're swirled through the bushes behind the shopping centre car park where I fumblingly lost my virginity to Janey Wilton. Twigs tear and bloody my face. I'm infatuated but she hasn't come near me since.

There's Dunstan in a confusion of bubbles. The look on his face!

The current sweeps us up the street to Darryl's house. We slam into each other as we're forced through the door. The tanks are ripped from my back. Furniture and belongings are in disarray, somersaulting. A beanbag and a fondue set roll past. The wave knows where to go. Arms flail as it roils us up the passageway. Shoulder blades scrape past the door jamb as we're squeezed into the bedroom next to Darryl's. The water calms and we stall, bobbing gently, limbs in a slow-motion ballet. Cheeks and eyes bulging. As we stare at each other my watch rises slowly from the side of the bed and hovers between us. Seconds before our lungs explode, my best friend fires an expression of hatred and betrayal at me.

We're in his brother's room.

But the horizon remains an undisturbed line. Darryl craves hair of the dog. As we trudge to the pub we pass Dunstan by the jetty. Darryl leans close. Hisses in my ear with a moue of distaste. 'Reckon it's true what they say about him?'

Later we stagger back to his place. His brother's hosing down the car. As we pass he stamps into a puddle. A splash hits the cuffs of my pants. I return his mischievous grin. Hold the stare a tad too long. Darryl's eyes narrow.

SEMAPHORE BEACH

Annette Willis

On a Moonless Night at Grange

David Adès

Tonight, the jetty has no end:
its wooden rails, bony arms outstretched,
vanish in darkness, sleepwalking west
across St Vincent Gulf.

I am here, at the city's edge, unmoored,
looking out to an invisible sea.
No distant flickering lights appear
on water or sky, no breeze touches skin,

no movement catches the eye.
The jetty is almost deserted:
only a lone fisherman dreams,
motionless beside his empty bucket.

I step out, feet sounding remote
on the boards, a narrow strip of bleached
wood unwinding. My body slows,
slips into the rhythm of the whoosh

and murmur of unseen waves.
I drift into sleep, walk sixty-five kilometres
along these weathered planks,
wake up on the shore of Yorke Peninsula.

Author Biographies

David Adès has published poetry widely since 1988. His poems appear in the CD *Adelaide 9, The Poetry of the City*. His first collection of poetry, *Mapping the World*, was launched in March 2008.

Jude Aquilina has lived in Adelaide all her life and has published two collections of poetry with Wakefield Press: *Knifing the Ice* and *On a moon spiced night*.

Anne Bartlett grew up in rural South Australia and is married with four adult children. She has worked as editor, ghostwriter, humour columnist and biographer, and is now concentrating on fiction.

Courtney Black was born in Adelaide in 1980. Her poems have been published in Friendly Street Poets/Wakefield Press's *New Poets 13*, and in a range of other anthologies and literary journals.

Ken Bolton works at the Experimental Art Foundation in Adelaide, South Australia. He writes poetry and art criticism. He does a little publishing via Little Esther Books and also runs the Lee Marvin Readings.

Gillian Britton's short stories have most recently been published in *Meanjin*, *Island* and *Wet Ink*. She is currently working towards a PhD in Creative Writing at the University of Adelaide.

Shannon Burns grew up in Adelaide and has lived there all his life. He is married and has a son.

Larry Buttrose grew up in Adelaide. A poet, playwright, novelist and nonfiction author, his new book, *From Eden to Eldorado: Tales of the Popes*, will be published in 2009.

Rob de Kok is a writer/director previously published by Heinemann, QUP and Friendly Street Poets. His films have screened at the Adelaide Film Festival and on the ABC. He teaches at Rosebud Writing Workshops in the Adelaide Hills.

John De Laine has been writing poetry since 1995, so he ought to know how to do it by now. You be the judge.

Kate Deller Evans – After years lecturing at Flinders University and ACA, Kate now runs *The Write Coach* business. She's a published poet and is currently working on four verse and fantasy novels. http://www.sawc.org.au/authors/kate-deller-evans.html

Ed Douglas is a well-known photographer and art educator who established the BAVA photography course at the SA School of Art. His work is in several major Australian collections, including the AGSA, AGNSW and the NGA.

Steve Evans has published eleven books, including *Taking Shape* (2004), and the history/anthology of the Friendly Street Poets, *Best of Friends* (with Kate Deller-Evans, 2008). He is an international literary editor and teaches at Flinders University.

Petra Fromm is a nonfiction editor for *Wet Ink: the magazine of new writing*. She lives and writes in inner-suburban Adelaide.

Cameron Fuller is currently working on a PhD in Creative Writing at UniSA. His poetry volume, *Low background noise*, was published in *Friendly Street New Poets 11*.

John Griffin is a retired English teacher. He has written poems (hundreds), short stories (dozens) and fourteen radio plays. His story 'The Satisfying Summer of Burton Yglesias' won the 2007 Alan Marshall prize.

Rachel Hennessy has lived in both small and big cities, including Canberra, Newcastle, Brisbane, Sydney, London and, currently, Adelaide. Her first novel, *The Quakers*, published by Wakefield Press in March 2008, was described by writer John Birmingham as 'unputdownable'.

Jill Jones won the 2003 Kenneth Slessor Poetry Prize for *Screens Jets Heaven*. In 2007 she was a featured poet at the 23rd Festival International de la Poésie in Trois-Rivières, Canada.

Nicholas Jose has published novels, short stories, essays and a memoir. He held the Chair of Creative Writing at the University of Adelaide, 2005–2008, and is now with the Writing and Society Research Group at the University of Western Sydney.

Cath Kenneally has published *Harmers Haven*, *Around Here* (which won the John Bray National Poetry Prize), *All Day All Night*, *Ci Vediamo* and in 2009 a fifth poetry collection. Her first novel, *Room Temperature*, is being followed by *Holmwood* next year.

Stephen Lawrence has three published collections of poetry, and is working towards a PhD in Creative Writing. He has been a judge for the Adelaide Festival Literary Awards from 2002 to 2008.

Carol Lefevre is a graduate of the University of Adelaide's Creative Writing programme. Her novel, *Nights in the Asylum*, was shortlisted for the Commonwealth Writers Prize and won the 2008 Nita B Kibble Award. She lives in Adelaide.

Brunette Lenkić grew up in a bountiful garden in Adelaide's northeastern suburbs. She now lives in Perth with her family and an immature fig tree.

Mary Manning is a Melbourne writer. She works in magazine editing after a long career in education. Her favourite excursion is to Adelaide for Writers' Week.

Amy T Matthews has a PhD in Creative Writing from the University of Adelaide. She is a teacher, writer and toddler-wrangler; she dreams of running away to join the circus where she will wear feathers in her hair and ride an elephant. Preferably a pink elephant. Which she will name Eudora. Unless it's a boy. Then it will be called Kevin.

David Mortimer is working on a third collection of poetry, for which he has received Arts SA support. Mortimer believes poetry should entertain the eye, the ear, the mouth and the mind.

Stephen Orr's first novel, *Attempts to Draw Jesus*, described the disappearance of two jackaroos in the Great Sandy Desert in 1987. He writes columns for News Ltd papers, *New Matilda* and other journals. His third novel won the SA Premiers' Award for an Unpublished MS at the Adelaide Festival in 2008.

Graham Rowlands is an Adelaide-based poet who has published very widely in Australian magazines, newspapers and anthologies since the late 1960s.

Harvey Schiller is a photographer and digital artist living in Adelaide. A prolific creator of images, he has exhibited successfully at a number of local galleries.

Angela Smith's poetry has been published widely in literary journals and has been displayed in Melbourne trains. She has been awarded two Young Adult Fiction Residencies at Varuna – The Writers' House.

Bernadette Smith is a PhD candidate in Creative Writing at the University of Adelaide. She has been published in *Island* and *Hecate*.

Anna Solding often falls asleep while reading bedtime stories to her sons. Even so, reading is one of her passions alongside writing and travelling. Tutoring and editing help pay the bills.

Heather Taylor Johnson moved from America to Adelaide in 1999. She holds a PhD in Creative Writing from the University of Adelaide, is a poetry editor for *Wet Ink* magazine and reviews poetry and other artforms for various publications. Her first poetry collection, *Exit Wounds*, was published by Picaro Press in 2007.

Kristel Thornell has published fiction, poetry and reviews in several journals. A PhD candidate at the University of Adelaide, she is currently writing a novel in upstate New York.

John Tranter is an honorary associate in the School of Letters, Arts and Media at the University of Sydney, and an honorary fellow of the Australian Academy of the Humanities. He is completing a doctorate at the University of Wollongong, and manages *Jacket* magazine.

Colin Varney has written for a pants-shy bear ('Here's Humphrey') and for disembodied lips ('Mulligrubs'). He was a drummer/lyricist for Adelaide bands Les Goolies and Ugly Ugly Ugly, and is a current contributor to *The Adelaide Review*. Deeply nerdy, his writing personal best is being published in *Doctor Who Magazine*.

Alexandra Weaver was born in South Australia in 1982. She has a Master of Arts in Creative Writing from the University of Adelaide and is currently at work on a novel entitled *The End of Knowing Everything*.

Annette Willis won the 2006 Wollongong City Gallery Portraiture Prize. She has been a finalist in the Head On Portrait Prize and her work was exhibited in London for the London Photographic Awards 2007.

Michael Winkler is a Melbourne writer and frequent Adelaide visitor. He has had short stories published in several literary magazines and the Penguin anthology *Sunset*. His website is www.michaelwinkler.com.au.

Wakefield Press is an independent publishing and
distribution company based in Adelaide, South Australia.
We love good stories and publish beautiful books.
To see our full range of titles, please visit our website at
www.wakefieldpress.com.au.